EDITED BY
SALLY SHELDON AND
KAYE WELLINGS

DECRIMINALISING ABORTION IN THE UK

What Would It Mean?

T0339264

POLICY PRESS SHORTS POLICY & PRACTICE

First published in Great Britain in 2020 by

Policy Press
University of Bristol
1-9 Old Park Hill
Bristol
BS2 8BB
UK
t: +44 (0)117 954 5940
pp-info@bristol.ac.uk
www.policypress.co.uk

North America office:
Policy Press
c/o The University of Chicago Press
1427 East 60th Street
Chicago, IL 60637, USA
t: +1 773 702 7700
f: +1 773-702-9756
sales@press.uchicago.edu
www.press.uchicago.edu

Selection, editorial matter and introduction © Sally Sheldon and Kaye Wellings 2020

Individual chapters © their respective authors 2020

British Library Cataloguing in Publication Data
A catalogue record for this book is available from the British Library

Library of Congress Cataloging-in-Publication Data
A catalog record for this book has been requested

ISBN 978-1-4473-5401-7 paperback
ISBN 978-1-4473-5403-1 ePub
ISBN 978-1-4473-5402-4 ePdf

The right of Sally Sheldon and Kaye Wellings to be identified as editors of this work has been asserted by them in accordance with the Copyright, Designs and Patents Act 1988.

The statements and opinions contained within this publication are solely those of the editors and contributors and not of the University of Bristol or Policy Press. The University of Bristol and Policy Press disclaim responsibility for any injury to persons or property resulting from any material published in this publication.

Policy Press works to counter discrimination on grounds of gender, race, disability, age and sexuality.

Cover design by David Worth
Front cover image: Alamy
Printed and bound in Great Britain by CMP, Poole
Policy Press uses environmentally responsible print partners

Contents

List of figures and tables

Figures

Tables

List of cases, statutes and statutory instruments

Cases

Non-UK cases

Statutes

Non-UK statutes

Statutory instruments

Notes on contributors

Marie Fox holds the Queen Victoria Chair of Law, in the School of Law and Social Justice at the University of Liverpool and is Associate Dean for Research and Impact. She has previously worked at the Universities of Lancaster, Queen's Belfast, Manchester, Keele and Birmingham. Her research is concerned with the legal governance of human and animal bodies, legal conceptions of embodiment and regulation of reproduction. Current projects (funded by the Dunhill Medical Trust, Wellcome Trust and Socio-legal Studies Association) focus on pet loss and the place of companion animals in care homes, governance of assisted reproductive technologies, and abortion law reform in Northern Ireland.

Ann Marie Gray is Professor of Social Policy at Ulster University and Co-Director of ARK (Access Research Knowledge, www.ark.ac.uk), a joint Ulster University and Queen's University Belfast research centre. She has published on devolution and policymaking, including health and social care and the governance of welfare. She is a Fellow of the Academy of Social Sciences.

Jonathan Herring is Professor of Law at the Faculty of Law, University of Oxford and DM Wolfe-Clarendon Fellow in Law at Exeter College, University of Oxford.

Goretti Horgan is a lecturer in Social Policy at Ulster University and Policy Director of ARK (Access Research Knowledge, www.ark.ac.uk). She was the Principal Investigator on a study that investigated the social harm of criminalisation of abortion in Northern Ireland, which was funded by the Economic and Social Research Council through its Transformative Research Programme.

Emily Jackson is Professor of Law at the London School of Economics and Political Science, where she teaches Medical Law. She is a Fellow of the British Academy, and was previously a member and then deputy chair of the Human Fertilisation & Embryology Authority, and a Judicial Appointments Commissioner. In 2017, she was awarded an OBE for services to higher education.

Brooke Ronald Johnson Jr, PhD, is an anthropologist who coordinated research and technical support on safe abortion and post-abortion contraception at Ipas (1990–2005), an international organisation that addresses reproductive health services, access to services and fulfillment of reproductive rights, and the World Health Organization, Department of Reproductive Health and Research (2005–2019, retired). Career highlights include: coordinating national strategic assessments, research and policy and service-delivery interventions on abortion in Africa, Asia and Eastern Europe; playing a central role in the 2012 revision and dissemination of the WHO *Safe abortion: technical and policy guidance for health systems*; conceptualising and leading the development of the WHO/HRP/UN Global Abortion Policies Database; providing WHO testimony to the Oireachtas Parliamentary Committee on the Eighth Amendment to the Irish Constitution; and serving as Chair of the WHO Research Ethics Review Committee and WHO Public Health Ethics Consultation Group.

Louise Keogh is a health sociologist in the Melbourne School of Population and Global Health at the University of

Melbourne, where she is an associate professor. She researches lay and expert perceptions of risk and health decision-making, particularly in relation to the use of health technology (for example, contraception, abortion, genetic testing, cancer screening). She is an expert in qualitative research methodology and the translation of evidence to clinical practice, and an award-winning teacher.

Patricia A. Lohr is the Medical Director of the British Pregnancy Advisory Service. She is a founding member and the education lead of the British Society of Abortion Care Providers, Abortion Education Adviser to the Royal College of Obstetricians and Gynaecologists (RCOG), chair of the Expert Working Group on the specialised commissioning of termination of pregnancy for patients with complex co-morbidities, and an associate editor for the journal *BMJ Sexual & Reproductive Health*. She is a Fellow of the American Congress of Obstetricians and Gynecologists and the Society of Family Planning. She was awarded an honorary fellowship from the Faculty of Sexual and Reproductive Healthcare in 2015 and was admitted as Fellow ad Eundem to the RCOG in 2018.

Jonathan Lord, MD, FRCOG, is a consultant gynaecologist and the Medical Director of Marie Stopes International UK. He is co-chair of the British Society of Abortion Care Providers (BSACP) and of the Royal College of Obstetricians and Gynaecologists (RCOG) abortion taskforce. He is the NHS clinician representative on the National Institute for Health and Care Excellence (NICE) clinical guideline and quality standards committees on abortion care. He also has clinical and academic interests in ambulatory gynaecology (for example, menstrual disorder) and fertility (for example, polycystic ovary syndrome).

Wendy V. Norman, MD, MHSc, CCFP, FCFP, DTM&H, is a family physician-researcher. She holds the Chair in Family Planning Public Health Research from the Canadian

Institutes of Health Research and Public Health Agency of Canada; is an associate professor in the Faculty of Medicine, University of British Columbia, in Canada; and an honorary associate professor in the Faculty of Public Health and Policy at the London School of Hygiene & Tropical Medicine in the UK. In 2015, Dr Norman was awarded the prestigious Guttmacher Darroch Award for advancing reproductive health policy research. She founded and leads the Canadian national collaboration: Contraception and Abortion Research Team (www.cart-grac.ca).

Sam Rowlands is a visiting professor at Bournemouth University. He is the editor of *Abortion Care*, published in 2014 by Cambridge University Press. He has been Secretary of the British Society of Abortion Care Providers since its inception in 2015. He is a Fellow of both the Royal College of General Practitioners and the Faculty of Sexual and Reproductive Health Care.

Sally Sheldon is Professor of Law at the University of Kent and University of Technology, Sydney. She is a trustee of the Abortion Support Network, a former trustee of the British Pregnancy Advisory Service and a Fellow of the Academy of Social Sciences. She is currently completing a major AHRC-funded study of the Abortion Act (1967).

Kaye Wellings is Professor of Sexual and Reproductive Health Research at the London School of Hygiene and Tropical Medicine. Wellings was a founder of the National Survey of Sexual Attitudes and Lifestyles. She led the first global study of sexual behaviour and has carried out evaluations of several national sexual and reproductive health interventions, including England's Teenage Pregnancy Strategy. She is an elected Fellow of the Faculty of Public Health, of the Faculty of Sexual and Reproductive Health, of the Royal College of Obstetricians and Gynaecologists and of the Academy of Social Sciences.

ONE

Introduction

Sally Sheldon and Kaye Wellings

Introduction

When people talk about the 'abortion question', what they generally mean is something like this: how should we balance the protection of unborn human life against the rights and interests of a pregnant woman to control her own body? Possibly, they also have in mind a further important (but analytically distinct) issue: how should law (criminal or otherwise) be deployed to enforce the answer given to the first question?

These are important moral and – for some – theological questions. However, this book does not engage directly with either of them. Rather, it aims to clear the waters, allowing them to be discussed in a way that is unmuddied by myths and misconceptions regarding matters of fact. In a debate where seemingly even the most basic empirical claims are disputed, the book offers a clear and succinct account of the relevant evidence. Where does public opinion stand with regard to the permissibility of abortion? What would be the likely impact of decriminalisation on women's health? Would it remove unnecessary restrictions on best clinical practice resulting in the improvement of services, or would it rather amount to dangerous deregulation, removing essential safeguards against harmful practice? Would unqualified backstreet providers be left at liberty to offer unsafe services? Would it remain possible to punish those who cause women to lose wanted pregnancies through vicious assaults? And what lessons can we learn from the experience of other countries regarding the role played by criminal prohibitions on abortion and the likely impact of their removal?

While different people hold profoundly diverging views regarding the morality of abortion, the answers to these kinds of questions should not be a matter of moral disagreement. Rather, each can be answered through reference to robust clinical trials, well conducted observational studies, detailed consideration of demographic data, rigorous opinion polls, and careful analysis of relevant law. In the chapters to follow, the authors take on this work. They navigate a field in which high quality peer-reviewed studies, the findings of expert committees and data obtained from rigorous, representative opinion polls rub shoulders with ideologically driven pseudo-science, misleading lobbying literature, unsubstantiated media reports, personal anecdotes, and opinion data generated by 'push-polling'. All too frequently in public debate, claims that cite these various sources are wrongly offered up as if they have equivalent weight. Here, the authors sift and evaluate the evidence to offer a robust response to each of the questions discussed earlier, relying on the best available evidence. The aim is to ensure that readers are fully informed on these important questions of fact before they reach their own view on the moral issues at the heart of the abortion debate.

This introductory chapter begins by briefly explaining what is meant by the 'decriminalisation' of abortion, before outlining the relevant current law. It then moves on to offer an overview of trends in the incidence of abortion in the UK and how these have been shaped by broad demographic factors and sexual and reproductive health policy. Finally, the chapter considers how reform might come about and what form it might take, before briefly introducing the five chapters to follow.

What do we mean by 'decriminalisation' of abortion?

In July 2019, *Time* magazine was forced to revise the headline that it had given to an earlier article, which had wrongly claimed that the Abortion Act 1967 had decriminalised abortion in England, Wales and Scotland (Haynes, 2019). The author of the original headline can, perhaps, be forgiven: he or she was far from alone in holding this mistaken belief. In a recent poll conducted by ICM, 69 per cent of the 2,002 people surveyed believed that abortion was currently 'completely legal if the woman requests it', with only 13 per cent identifying the correct legal position: that abortion is a 'criminal act unless certain strict conditions are met' (ICM, 2017).

For the purposes of this book, 'decriminalisation of abortion' is understood to mean the removal of those specific prohibitions that render abortion a criminal act, punishing the intentional ending of a pregnancy either by a woman herself or by a third party. Decriminalisation of abortion can be either partial (for example, where criminal penalties are removed only within a prescribed time period, say the first 24 weeks of pregnancy) or full (where no specific criminal prohibitions are retained at any stage of pregnancy).

We should also be clear about what 'decriminalisation' does not mean. Notably, following decriminalisation, the performance of abortions would not be exempt from criminal law: as will be described in Chapter Four, general criminal offences that apply to all medical treatment would continue to apply to non-consensual or dangerously negligent procedures. Nor does decriminalisation necessarily mean that there should be no specific regulation of abortion, merely that any such specific regulation should not be backed by criminal sanction. For example, while reporting of female genital mutilation is now mandatory in the UK, failure to report attracts not a criminal sanction but a disciplinary one, enforced by the relevant professional regulatory organisation, such as the General Medical Council (section 5B, *Female Genital Mutilation Act* 2003). Likewise, when the Australian state of Victoria decriminalised abortion, it laid down specific requirements that must be met in order for an abortion to be performed after 24 weeks but backed them with a professional sanction, rather than a criminal one (see Chapter Six).

Current law in the UK

What are the specific criminal prohibitions that punish the intentional ending of a pregnancy? These are to be found in a number of statutes and common law provisions, which together constitute the oldest extant statutory framework governing any specific medical procedure (Sheldon, 2016). The law differs in significant ways between England and Wales, Scotland and Northern Ireland.

The Offences Against the Person Act (1861)

The Offences Against the Person Act 1861 applies in England, Wales and Northern Ireland. It is a product of mid-Victorian Britain: in the memorable words of Sir James Munby, subsequently President of the Family Division of the High Court and a member of the Court of Appeal, it was passed at a time when 'our society was only on the brink of the beginnings of the modern world' (*Smeaton* 2002: para 332). While excluding the abortion provisions from its recent review of the Offences Against the Person Act, the Law Commission of England and Wales found generally that the statute was 'outdated' and 'notoriously difficult to understand and use', noting that it relies on 'archaic and obscure' language and that its offences are poorly defined and incoherently classified (Law Commission, 2015).

The Offences Against the Person Act creates two specific abortion offences: 'unlawful procurement of miscarriage' (section 58) and supplying or procuring an instrument or 'poison or other noxious thing', knowing that it is intended to be used to procure a miscarriage (section 59). A third, related offence of concealment of birth allows a woman to be charged where infanticide or late abortion is suspected but cannot be proven. Apart from some minor changes in available sentences, these provisions have survived largely unaltered since 1861. While in many countries, women are exempt from prosecution for inducing the miscarriage of their own pregnancies, the Offences Against the Person Act offences apply to the pregnant woman who self-induces a miscarriage as well as to a third-party abortionist. They draw no distinction between abortions earlier and later in pregnancy, thus capturing any procedure that occurs after implantation (six to twelve days after fertilisation). Under section 58, both women and third parties face the harshest potential penalty for abortion foreseen in any European country (Nebel and Hurka, 2015): life imprisonment.

The Offences Against the Person Act makes no explicit provision for therapeutic abortion, leaving doctors potentially liable for the same offence as unqualified abortionists. However, a creative judicial interpretation of section 58, offered in the case of *Bourne*, provided that abortion would be lawful where performed by a doctor in order to 'preserve a woman's life', with this phrase interpreted broadly to include cases where a termination might prevent her from becoming 'a mental or physical wreck' (*Bourne* 1938: 619). Until October 2019, this highly ambiguous test remained the legal basis for the very small number of lawful abortions performed within Northern Ireland each year, where it was restrictively interpreted, particularly in more recent years (Women and Equalities Committee, 2019: para 12; Chapter Five). However, Northern Irish abortion law was found to breach human rights norms, with the Committee on the Elimination of Discrimination Against Women recommending that fundamental reform of the law was necessary to render it human rights compliant (CEDAW, 2018; see generally Chapter Five). In July 2019, Parliament voted by an overwhelming majority for the government to introduce regulations to implement CEDAW's recommendations should the Northern Ireland Executive not be re-established by 21 October 2019. When this date passed with no change at Stormont, sections 58 and 59 were repealed for Northern Ireland and a moratorium was introduced on any prosecutions under them. At the time of going to press, the government is consulting on how abortion services should be introduced and regulated within Northern Ireland.

These offences are prosecuted infrequently. In recent years, section 58 appears to have been charged most often in cases where a wanted pregnancy is lost as the result of an assault on a pregnant woman or following the non-consensual administration of abortifacients (Sheldon, 2016). However, a small number of prosecutions have also been brought against women in England who have self-induced miscarriages very late in their pregnancies (for example, *Catt* 2013), and against women in Northern Ireland, who terminated early pregnancies using pills acquired on the internet (Women and Equalities Committee, 2019; Chapter Five).

The Infant Life (Preservation) Act (1929) and Criminal Justice Act NI (1945)

A second statute, the Infant Life (Preservation) Act 1929, applies in England and Wales. Its terms are replicated in section 25 of the Criminal Justice Act (Northern Ireland) 1945. These statutes prohibit the intentional destruction of 'the life of a child capable of being born alive … before it has an existence independent of its mother', unless this is done 'in good faith for the purpose only of preserving the life of the mother'. Each statute contains a rebuttable presumption that capacity for life is acquired at 28 weeks of gestation, reflecting the state of neonatal medicine in the 1920s. Subsequent advances mean that this presumption is today likely to be considered to have been rebutted, with viability accepted to be reached some weeks earlier (Science and Technology Committee, 2007; Chapter Two). Again, this offence has been charged infrequently and then generally in the context of assaults against pregnant women. It overlaps with the offence of 'unlawful procurement of miscarriage' under section 58 of the Offences Against the Person Act, offering an alternative charge where pregnancy has reached an advanced gestation. These statutes also foresee a potential sanction of life imprisonment. They do not apply to Scotland, where abortion remains an offence at common law (Gordon, 1967; McKnorrie, 1985).

The 2019 reform of Northern Irish abortion law did not include repeal of section 25 of the Criminal Justice Act. As such, it remains a serious criminal offence to end the life of child 'capable of being born alive'.

The Abortion Act (1967)

The Abortion Act 1967 applies in England, Wales and Scotland but not in Northern Ireland. It exempts those who conform to its requirements from prosecution under the abortion offences described earlier. The Act is a product of the moral climate and clinical realities of the 1960s, when widespread backstreet abortions resulted in significant maternal mortality and morbidity (Birkett, 1939; Dickens, 1966; Lane, 1974a). Abortion was then a far riskier, more technically demanding, surgical procedure which required the skilled hand of a doctor and, on average, a stay of over one week in hospital (Chapter Three; Lane, 1974a: table D4; Lane, 1974b: table 5.1).

These clinical realities were reflected in the restrictions contained in the Abortion Act. The Act was intended to ensure 'that socially acceptable abortions should be carried out under the safest conditions attainable', 'with all proper skill and in hygienic conditions' (*RCN* 1981: 575 and 569). It provides that, in order to avoid a criminal offence, three conditions must be met. First, two doctors must certify in good faith that an abortion is justified on the basis of one or more of the four broad grounds set out under the Act:

a) continuance of the pregnancy would involve greater risk than termination to the physical or mental health of the pregnant woman or existing children of her family (subject to a 24-week limit);

b) termination is necessary to prevent grave permanent injury to the physical or mental health of the pregnant woman;

c) continuance of the pregnancy would involve greater risk than would termination to the life of the pregnant woman; or

d) there is a substantial risk that if the child were born it would suffer from 'such physical or mental abnormalities as to be seriously handicapped'.

In determining whether the first two conditions are met, the doctors may take account of the pregnant woman's 'actual or reasonably foreseeable environment' (section 1(2)).

Second, the abortion must be performed by a registered medical practitioner, meaning that a doctor must 'accept responsibility' for the procedure (*RCN* 1981: 569–70, 575, 577). And, third, it must be performed on NHS or other approved premises, with this requirement underpinning specific licensing requirements on non-NHS service providers (see Chapter Four). Since 1990, the government has had the power to license a broader 'class of places' – such as GPs' surgeries or women's homes – for the performance of abortions performed using medicines rather than surgery (see Chapter Three). In an emergency situation, the requirements for two signatures and for an abortion to be performed in NHS or approved premises do not apply (section 1(4)).

The Abortion Act also affords healthcare professionals a statutory right of 'conscientious objection', whereby they can refuse to participate in treatment authorised under the Act (section 4). Further, it requires the notification of all abortions certified and performed, underpinning the publication of detailed annual abortion statistics (section 2). The Abortion Act does not make any provision for informed consent, counselling or safeguarding. Nor does it offer protection from intimidation or harassment of those accessing services, with the Court of Appeal having recently recognised that such conduct can cause 'significant emotional and psychological damage' to some (*Dulgheriu* 2019).

In sum, UK abortion law is very old. It is characterised by unclear and archaic language, overlapping offences and harsh sentences. The relevant offences are very rarely prosecuted. While the Abortion Act was intended to ensure that abortions were performed by appropriately skilled professionals in hygienic conditions, it was passed at a time of very different clinical realities and social mores. Further, the basis for important protections of those who access services are to be found not within this framework but in general provisions of law (see Chapter Four).

We now turn to consider how abortion services have developed within this legal framework. How do abortion rates within the UK compare to those in other western nations? And how have they changed over time?

Reproductive and sexual health in the UK

Since the Abortion Act came into effect, abortion has become an increasingly widely accepted part of life (see Chapter Two). One in three women in the UK has an abortion in her lifetime and roughly one in five pregnancies end in abortion (Wellings et al, 2013). Around 200,000 abortions a year take place in England and Wales, with another 13,000 in Scotland. Roughly 5 per cent of the total are on non-resident women, although in recent years the vast majority of these have travelled from either the Republic of Ireland or Northern Ireland (DHSC, 2019a), meaning that this proportion is likely to decrease significantly in light of the recent liberalisation of the law in each of those places. Both the numbers of abortions carried out and rates per 1,000 women of reproductive age have fluctuated over time. Routinely collected statistics showed a sharp increase in the reported abortion rate following the 1967 Abortion Act, which made it a criminal offence not to report abortions. As a result, for the first time, reliable statistics were available on the number of abortions carried out in Britain. What the official statistics showed unequivocally was the marked fall after the 1967 Act in infections and mortality resulting from illegal abortions (see Chapter Three).

The rate of increase in reported abortions slowed from the early 1970s and actually fell from 1991 to 1995, possibly reflecting a more conservative attitude towards sexual behaviour generally in the era of widespread fear of AIDS and HIV transmission. Since the mid-1990s the abortion rate has been relatively stable in England and Wales (Figure 1.1), though there has been a very recent hike in the figures. In every 1,000 resident women of reproductive age, 17.4 had an abortion in 2018 compared with 16.7 in 2017, taking the rate back to its level in 2008 (DHSC, 2019a). Rates for Scotland remain

Figure 1.1: Age standardised abortion rate per 1,000 women aged 15–44, England and Wales, 1970 to 2018

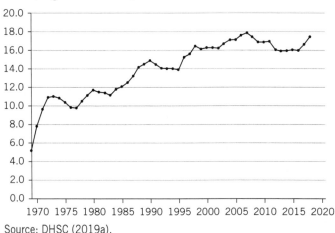

Source: DHSC (2019a).

Figure 1.2: Abortion rate per 1,000 women by age, England and Wales, 2008 and 2018

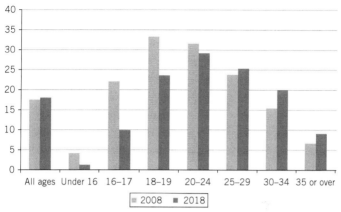

Source: DHSC (2019a).

lower, while also hitting a ten year high in 2018, at 12.9 per 1,000 women (ISD, 2019).

Within the overall trends there are marked age differences (Figure 1.2). The abortion rate is highest among 20 to 24 year-olds and has changed less in this age group over the last decade, while rates among younger women have fallen year on year. The under-18 rate in 2018 of 8.1 per 1,000 women was less than half the 2008 rate of 18.9 per 1,000. Conversely, rates have been increasing among older women. The rate for women aged 35 and over was 9.2 per 1,000 in 2018, compared with 6.7 in 2008 (DHSC, 2019a). These same broad trends are visible in Scotland (ISD, 2019).

The majority of abortions are certified under the statutory ground of risk of harm to the mental or physical health of the pregnant woman. Only 2 per cent are the result of doctors deciding that there was a substantial risk that if the child were born it would suffer from such physical or mental abnormalities as to be seriously handicapped. Of abortions in England and Wales, 71 per cent were medically as opposed to surgically induced in 2018, an increase on the 2017 figure of 66 per cent and almost double the proportion in 2008 (37 per cent). In Scotland, the figure was even higher: 86.1 per cent of abortions reported in 2018 were performed using medicines (ISD, 2019). An increasingly large proportion of abortions take place in the first trimester, with nine out of ten abortions carried out under 13 weeks. Since the advent of medical abortion, higher proportions of procedures have been carried out very early in the pregnancy: four out of five abortions were carried out under 10 weeks in 2018 (DHSC, 2019a; ISD, 2019). Contrary to the impression given in some media reports, late abortions are rare. Fewer than 2 per cent happen after 20 weeks, and these tend to be for particularly serious reasons (Nevill, 2017).

The abortion rate can be seen as an indicator of reproductive health. Strategic options for preventing unintended pregnancy occupy a continuum. At the start of the reproductive process they include methods of preventing ovulation by, for example, use of combined hormonal contraception. Where an egg has already been released, use of barrier methods of contraception and hormonal methods aimed at creating a hostile environment for the male sperm will prevent fertilisation. In the event that fertilisation has occurred, use of emergency contraception can prevent implantation. Finally, where an unintended pregnancy is already underway, medical or surgical methods of abortion can be used to end it. The earlier in this process that measures can be taken to prevent an unintended pregnancy, the better for the woman involved, the lower the costs to the NHS, and the lesser the scope for controversy. Any increase in abortion rates may reflect an unmet need for contraception.

Yet changes in the rates need also to be seen against the backcloth of recent demographic and social trends in Britain. There has been a progressive decrease over the past half century in age at onset of sexual activity, from a median of 20 for women born in the 1950s to a median of 16 for those born after 1990 (Wellings et al, 2013), and a parallel increase in the average age at which childbearing begins, from 23 years in 1967 to 28.8 years in 2018 (ONS, 2019c). During the interval between these events, now averaging almost a decade and a half, women are single (defined as neither married nor cohabiting), sexually active and not wanting to conceive. The trend towards smaller families and the consequent need to space births and avoid further pregnancies following completion of childbearing has further led to an appreciable extension of the period during which women are potentially at risk of unintended pregnancy. Taking the average age of sexual initiation, 16 years, as the starting point and age 49 as the reproductive end-point, women now spend some 30 years of their lives avoiding unwanted pregnancy (ONS, 2019c).

Given these trends, it is surprising perhaps that the abortion rate in recent decades has remained relatively stable. In many respects, Britain can boast of being a success story in terms of national reproductive health and this is in large part due to contraception provision being free of charge under the NHS. While over half of pregnancies in Britain are planned, roughly one in six pregnancies are unplanned, and between a quarter and a third are categorised as ambivalent (Wellings et al, 2013). However, estimates from other high-income countries are higher. In France and the US, a third of pregnancies are estimated to be unplanned, two in five in Spain, and almost half in Japan (Wellings et al, 2013). Considerable success has also been achieved in relation to teenage conception. Conception rates for women aged under 18 years in England and Wales hit a record low in 2017 – declining by 60 per cent from 49.8 per 1,000 women in 1998 to 17.9 per 1,000 in 2017 (ONS, 2019a), the lowest rate recorded since comparable statistics were first produced in 1969. The fall in under 18 conceptions can be attributed to an increased time spent in education, investment in contraceptive services leading to improved uptake of reliable contraception, a change in social norms governing early motherhood, and investment in preventive programmes by successive governments, notably the Teenage

Pregnancy Strategy for England, 1999–2000 (ONS, 2016; Wellings et al, 2016).

Although most would probably consider abortion to be the least desirable of preventive options, sexual health policy in Britain supports its provision as part of the repertoire of strategies to reduce unintended births. Almost all abortions in Scotland, England and Wales are funded by the NHS. Whereas in Scotland, almost all are provided within the NHS, in England and Wales, the majority – 72 per cent – take place in the independent sector. Recognition that abortion provision is a key plank of reproductive health service provision in Britain has been reflected in successive policy documents (DH, 2013; PHE, 2015). Though not always escaping controversy, such guidance accepts the critical role of legal abortion in protecting the health and wellbeing of women who conceive unintentionally.

How might decriminalisation of abortion come about in the UK and what would it look like?

Full or partial decriminalisation of abortion in the UK would recognise the important role that abortion has come to play in reproductive health policy. It would require reform of some or all of the laws described earlier, passed by the relevant Parliament. In the case of England and Wales, this would be Westminster. For Scotland, abortion is a devolved matter so any reform is a matter for Holyrood. Abortion is also a devolved issue in Northern Ireland so, similarly, it would generally fall to Stormont to legislate. However, as noted earlier in the chapter, with the Northern Irish Assembly suspended since early 2017 and abortion law in Northern Ireland found to breach human rights norms, the UK Parliament recently voted to decriminalise abortion in Northern Ireland (see further Chapter Five).

The fact that decriminalisation necessarily requires a process of statutory reform means that national Parliaments are free to shape a new law in whichever way they see fit (and this will also be true for Stormont, if and when an Executive is re-established). Important issues to be considered in this process include whether:

- to decriminalise abortion throughout pregnancy or just within certain gestational limits;
- to introduce specific new offences to prohibit non-consensual abortion; to revise existing offences that might do this work; or whether existing criminal law offences of assault and poisoning already offer sufficient protection (see Chapter Four);
- to retain specific statutory provision for conscientious objection and, if so, whether to include a statutory duty to ensure that women's timely access to services is not thereby impeded;
- to retain notification requirements;
- to make statutory provision for 'safe zones' around clinics, as has been done in some Australian jurisdictions, rather than leaving it to individual local authorities to apply for Public Space Protection Orders (*Dulgheriu* 2019).

One possible model of reform was foreseen in a Ten Minute Rule Bill, proposed by a cross-party group of MPs led by Diana Johnson (Abortion Bill 2017–19, HC Bill 276). This foresaw the repeal of sections 58–60 of the Offences Against the Person Act and the replacement of the existing abortion offences with two new offences that prohibited non-consensual abortion and abortion after 24 weeks. It retained provision for notification of abortions and protection for conscientious objection rights. Northern Ireland, where criminal prohibitions have been repealed, offers another model that might be extended elsewhere in the UK. Still other possibilities are offered by a number of Australian states that have recently decriminalised abortion, often removing offences modelled on those of UK law, and by Canada (see Chapter Six).

Content of the book

The rest of this book sets out the evidence that should inform debate regarding the repeal of specific criminal prohibitions against abortion. First, it explores the extent to which UK public opinion supports decriminalisation through a close analysis of available polling data (Chapter Two). It then moves on to assess the likely consequences for women's health of removing the legal restrictions imposed under the current criminal law framework (Chapter Three). This is followed by a legal analysis of whether decriminalisation is liable to result in a dangerous deregulation of services (Chapter Four). Given that the law there has evolved along different lines, Northern Ireland is treated separately, with Chapter Five exploring the impact of previous criminal abortion laws and the likely effects of their removal in the region. Finally, Chapter Six considers how the experience of other countries can inform our understanding of the potential consequences of decriminalisation of abortion, with a particular focus on two case studies that are frequently discussed in decriminalisation debates: Canada and Australia.

TWO

Is public opinion in support of decriminalisation?

Ann Marie Gray and Kaye Wellings

In this chapter we ask: how does the UK public view abortions? Is there support for removing specific criminal prohibitions against abortion? How does support vary with the grounds on which an abortion can be carried out? And what are the influences on public attitudes towards abortion? Public opinion in Northern Ireland is dealt with separately in this chapter since change in the legislative and policy-related backcloth in the past decade has been considerably more dramatic in that region than in the rest of the UK.

Introduction

Abortion tends to polarise debate as few social issues can. The subject combines emotive concepts of sex and death and raises fundamental questions about being human, such as when life begins. Abortion touches on many contentious issues, such as the right of women to control their own bodies; the responsibility of the state to protect the fetus; the tension between secular and religious views of human life; and the conflicting rights of the mother and the fetus (Weale et al,

2012). Also central to debates around abortion is whether the expression of sexuality should extend beyond procreation. Since there is still a residual view in western culture that the prime function of sex is procreation, discussion of abortion often leads to references to blame and retribution.

Can we rely on the polling evidence on attitudes towards abortion?

Any heated policy debate is generally accompanied by uses and misuses of statistics to support different sides of the argument. We rely on the findings of social research and opinion polls to access public views on an issue. Yet polling is an inexact science and often produces conflicting evidence. Gauging how and whether attitudes towards abortion have changed over time is made difficult by the fact that, at any one point in time and even within the same population, different surveys often produce different estimates. Over a three-year period between 2011 and 2013, British attitudes towards abortion were surveyed by two different agencies. Ipsos MORI (2006; 2011) showed a decline since the start of the century in support for abortion, while the National Centre for Social Research's British Social Attitudes Survey (BSA) showed an increase (BSA, 2015).

The inconsistencies in the findings are in large part attributable to differences in the research methods used. Findings vary according to the different issues referred to in survey questions: the moral status of the fetus, concerns relating to gestational age; autonomy, harm and possible negative consequences of allowing abortion; and the different reasons for abortion being carried out. The framing of questions is important in interpreting the findings, whether, for example, questions are asked from the perspective of a woman's rights to choose, the 'pro-choice' discourse, or from that of an unborn child's right to live, the 'pro-life' discourse. The labels 'pro-choice' and 'pro-life' both imply endorsement of strongly held values relating, respectively, to human agency and freedom on the one hand and to the right to and respect for life on the other. Hence they suggest to the respondent that to select the opposite response option in either case would indicate that they were 'anti-choice' or 'anti-life'. In a US poll carried out by the Public Religion Research Institute, seven in ten Americans described themselves as 'pro-choice' but almost as many described themselves as 'pro-life' (PRRI, 2019).

Even when questions appear to be neutrally framed, the phrasing can still be value-laden. For example, in describing human life before birth, terms such as 'baby' and 'child' are humanising and emotive, while terms such as 'embryo' and 'fetus' are more medical in connotation and likely to be seen as more neutral and objective. In the European Values survey carried out by TNS Sofres in 2005, respondents were asked: '[f]or each of the following sentences, tell me if they are very much, a little, not really or not at all in line with what you think'. Statements on which agreement/disagreement were sought included: '[i]f a woman doesn't want children, she should be able to have an abortion'. The question was – ostensibly – about a woman's rights, but the state of not wanting children may still have been perceived negatively by many, despite approximately one in five women in Britain remaining childless. Respondents may also have reacted by thinking that the woman should have used contraception if she wanted to avoid motherhood, and so the question introduces an element of culpability. All the same, a clear majority of 66 per cent agreed with the statement.

Reporting bias

Not only is polling an inexact science, it is also strongly politicised. Questions asked often reflect the views of the agencies commissioning them and are worded to elicit answers that validate the stance of those asking them. Survey researchers are familiar with an 'acquiescence bias', a tendency on the part of respondents to agree with a statement on which they are asked to express a view (Lavrakas, 2008). So if the attitudinal statements on which views are sought are all slanted in one particular direction, whether anti-abortion or pro-choice, the net result will be that the poll as a whole will be skewed in favour of one or other of these positions. In May 2017 ComRes carried out a survey on behalf of 'Where do they stand' (ComRes, 2017), which describes itself a grass-roots initiative that aims to inform public opinion regarding the views of their elected representatives on 'life issues'. The survey asked respondents to express their level of agreement with a number of statements related to abortion, which included the following:

- Criminal law plays an essential role in protecting patients against medical malpractice.
- Patients who are at serious risk of heavy bleeding due to a medical procedure or powerful drugs should have medical supervision, in person, from a doctor.
- Parental or guardian consent should be required for children aged 15 or under to undergo medical procedures or have powerful drugs administered with potentially serious side-effects.
- Parental or guardian consent should be required for girls aged 15 or under to undergo an abortion procedure.
- In Great Britain the upper time limit for abortion is 24 weeks or approximately six months' gestation. By comparison, in most other EU countries the limit for most abortions is 12 weeks or lower. In light of this difference what do you think the time limit should be in Britain?

Not surprisingly, a large majority of ComRes respondents endorsed the views expressed in each of the statements in the survey. Their formulation, however, breached accepted rules of research established to guard against bias. That is, the statements were all phrased to invite anti-abortion sentiment; they were not counterbalanced with a set of opposing opinions – a golden rule in social research to lessen agreement bias – and, by inference, several of them convey misinformation. The drugs used to bring about a medical abortion do not have serious side-effects (as we see in Chapter Three); effective medical regulations are in place via the General Medical Council to regulate the conduct of doctors without the need for criminal sanctions (as we see in Chapter Four); and there is already legally constituted guidance that a young woman under the age of medical consent but deemed competent may make a decision about having an abortion (RCGP, 2011; see Chapter Four). Reporting the ComRes results, *The Times* newspaper informed its readers: '[b]ecause we kill so many of our children, our ageing population is becoming unsustainable', adding '[t]he new ComRes poll shows most people agree and want the law tightened – not relaxed' (Macdonald, 2017). *Spectator* magazine columnist Melanie McDonagh claimed the results showed that public opinion was 'almost entirely at odds with the stance taken by most public broadcasters, pundits and parliamentarians' and declared that she would find the poll's findings 'very handy indeed' (McDonagh, 2017).

Further evidence of bias in reporting of polling results can be found in the fact that the same data, strategically selected, are often used to support diametrically opposing positions. Also in May 2017, the BBC ran a programme in which the views of a group of eight women with experience of abortion were compared with those of the wider British population, as captured in a linked ICM poll. The presenter quoted several results from the survey, including an apparent finding that the majority of people were in favour of abortion being decriminalised (Williams, 2017). The accuracy of this finding was contested by the MP for Congleton, Fiona Bruce, who accused the BBC of 'cherry-picking' polling results to reflect a particular lobby. She told the newspaper, the *Mail on Sunday*, 'How can people be expected to have a fair and proper debate if facts are suppressed?' The newspaper took up the MP's case, claiming that the programme had misled the public and that in fact the ICM showed that the majority of respondents did not support decriminalisation but 'strongly favour the current law of requiring two doctors to approve an abortion, over moves to weaken this' (Petrie and Adams, 2017). In fact, the BBC and the Mail on Sunday were both guilty of selective interpretation of the ICM findings. ICM had asked respondents: 'Do you think it is appropriate that abortion be considered a criminal matter?' to which 39 per cent said 'Yes', 34 per cent said 'No', and a relatively high proportion, 24 per cent, selected the 'Don't know' option (2 per cent answered that they preferred not to say). It was perhaps not surprising that such a high proportion selected the 'Don't know' option given responses to the previous question probing knowledge of the current legal situation, which revealed that only 13 per cent of respondents knew that abortion was 'a criminal act unless certain strict conditions are met, outside of which you can face life in prison' (ICM, 2017). So that while it was accurate to report that only a third thought it inappropriate to criminalise abortion, and little more than a third thought it not, it was inaccurate to claim that the remaining two thirds in each case supported either of the flip sides of these statements. To do so was to wrongly impute to the third of people who answered 'Don't know' an opinion they had not expressed.

Participation bias

A further issue determining the reliability of survey evidence is the sampling strategy. How robust the findings are depends greatly on how generalisable they are, that is, how accurately they represent the behaviour or attitudes of the wider population they aim to represent, which in turn depends on how the sample was selected and what proportion agree to take part. The 'gold standard' is random probability sampling, a technique which ensures that every member of the population, theoretically, has an equal chance of being picked to take part, increasing the chance that the results are representative of the entire population. This approach is expensive and time consuming, and so opinion polls such as ComRes and YouGov routinely use online platforms to deliver their surveys. A problem with online surveys is that there is no way of estimating the response rate, nor of determining whether those completing the survey differ from those who do not in ways that are important to the survey objectives.

The British Social Attitudes Survey

How then can we obtain a reliable picture of how Britain feels about abortion and the removal of specific criminal prohibitions against it? Of all the sources of data on attitudes to abortion in Britain, the most authoritative is the British Social Attitudes survey conducted by the National Centre for Social Research (Natcen) (BSA, 2015). Natcen is a charity and receives funding from mainly government sources and so is not swayed by the political or ideological persuasion of clients. The same questions have been asked for over 30 years, through successive changes of government. Repeating questions using the same wording and methodology means that changes over time can be charted. Natcen use random probability sampling in the BSA to interview 3,000 participants in their homes. A small number of questions about abortion have been asked since 1983. They do not specifically probe views on decriminalisation, but relevant questions ask about the acceptability of abortion under different circumstances:

Do you think the law should allow an abortion when:
… the woman's health is seriously endangered by the pregnancy?
… the woman decides on her own she does not wish to have the child?
… the couple cannot afford any more children?

The first question describes a situation laid down under the 1967 Abortion Act as one of the grounds on which two medical practitioners may deem it permissible for a woman to have an abortion – that a woman whose health is put at risk by her pregnancy should be allowed to have an abortion. The second question goes further than the 1967 Abortion Act, effectively describing a scenario that would exist if abortion were to be completely decriminalised and totally a matter of a woman's choice. (Note that the question refers specifically to the child the woman has currently conceived, and not more generally to having children in the future.) The third construes adverse effects of an ongoing pregnancy in terms, not of harm to health, but rather economic hardship. The different reasons given in the three scenarios have been variously categorised as traumatic (physical) or elective (social) reasons, for example, or as 'hard' or 'soft' reasons (Clements, 2014). The traumatic grounds concern risks to physical health of the expectant mother, serious fetal anomalies, or the pregnancy being the result of rape or incest. The elective reasons cover personal and familial circumstances, such as a family being socio-economically disadvantaged and not being able to afford to have a child. Previous research has shown that large majorities of public opinion favour abortion for 'hard' medical reasons, while opinion is more divided over abortion on 'soft' social or economic grounds.

The BSA data show that public attitudes vary with the reason for the abortion (Figure 2.1). Support for a woman's right to have an abortion if going ahead with the pregnancy would seriously endanger her health is near universal: 93 per cent of those sampled agreed with this view in 2017, a proportion barely changed from the 87 per cent who agreed in 1983. Support for the second scenario is lower, but still a clear majority hold the view that the law should allow abortion in situations where a woman does not want the child (70 per cent), a slightly higher proportion than think abortion should be allowed if a couple cannot afford any more children (65 per cent). This marks a considerable change since 1983, when only a minority (37 per cent) thought that the law

Figure 2.1: Proportion indicating the law should allow an abortion in different scenarios, 1983–2016

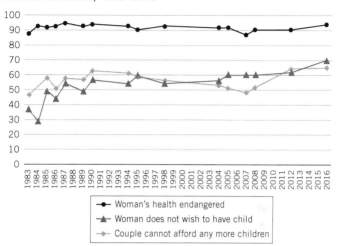

Source: Taylor, 2017.

should allow abortion because the woman did not want the child and the majority view (held by 55 per cent) was that it should not. In other words, just over half of the public in 1983 opposed abortion being available if a woman does not want a child – a figure which, by 2017, had fallen to less than a third.

Who is most accepting of decriminalisation of abortion? Evidence from the BSA

Analysis of the BSA data by different population groupings does not show significant variation in attitudes towards abortion by demographic characteristics. As is the case across many moral and social issues, younger people generally have more permissive views than older people, but they are only marginally more likely to approve of abortions on the basis simply that a woman does not wish to have the child. An interesting finding in the BSA relates to era in which people are born, as opposed to their age. Consistently across successive surveys, barely half of those born in the 1940s support abortion because a woman didn't want a child, compared with nearly three quarters of those born in the 1990s. Yet while overall support for abortion fell slightly from the mid-1990s to the end of the century, it continued to rise among those born during the 1950s. This may reflect the impact of the debates preceding the 1967 Abortion Act, which would have had a marked impact on the 1950s generation. The findings suggest that changes in attitudes seen since 1983 cannot only be explained by generational change but need to be examined in the context of historical era.

Although abortion is often characterised as a women's rights issue, the gender divide is less marked than might be expected. The BSA shows no significant differences between the sexes in their views on any of the scenarios asked about. This finding is consistent with evidence from studies elsewhere (Jelen 2015; Pew Research, 2018; Loll and Stidham Hall, 2019). Level of support for abortion generally increases with educational level. More than three quarters of graduates say abortion should be allowed if a woman does not want a child, compared with just over half of those with no formal qualifications. Support for abortion has, however, hardly changed among graduates since 1983, making them one of the few groups to have moved little in their views on the subject. Similarly, the BSA findings show few divisions on abortion by party political persuasion on abortion, except for a clear distinction between Liberal Democrat supporters (who are more likely to have more permissive views) and others.

By contrast, religion and religious identities are highly correlated with attitudes towards abortion. People who are not religious are the most accepting of abortion with nearly four out of five saying that a woman should be allowed by law to have an abortion if she does not wish to have the child. The relationship between religiosity and abortion attitudes has been widely studied elsewhere, with similar conclusions (Barkan, 2014; Adamczyk and Valdimarsdóttir, 2018).

There are some distinctions in attitudes held by different faith groups. Attitudes tend to reflect what are seen to be the prevailing views of religious leaders. Although the BSA data has consistently shown support for abortion if a woman doesn't want a child to be lower among Catholics compared with other religious groups, such support increased sharply between 1985 and 2017, almost doubling from one third to nearly two thirds. The sharp increase meant that, where previously, support for abortion had been lower among Catholics, by 2017 their views were more similar to those of the population as a whole. The shift in attitudes may have reflected the apparent relaxation of the Vatican's attitude towards abortion. Soon after becoming pontiff in 2013, Pope Francis appeared to be endorsing a softer stance towards issues such as abortion and homosexuality, saying that the Catholic Church must focus on 'compassion and mercy'. The leniency appeared short lived and, in 2018, the Pope told his weekly audience that it was 'not right' to take a human life, no matter how small. It is too soon to tell whether Pope Francis's revised position will have a further impact on the views of Catholics.

Many of the demographic factors influencing abortion, including age, gender, education and religion, interact with one another and this needs to be taken into account when interpreting the findings. The age effect, for example, may partly reflect the increasing proportion of the population receiving a university education. Similarly, the near-equal prevalence of support for abortion between men and women, which could seem counterintuitive given that women have more to gain from having autonomy over pregnancy outcome, may be explained by the fact that attitudes toward abortion are tied more closely to religion than gender. A possible reason for women not being found to be more supportive of abortion than men, is that they tend to be more religious than men.

Attitudes towards abortion in Northern Ireland

Public opinion has taken on far greater prominence in the rapidly moving debate about abortion law in Northern Ireland (NI) as those in favour of, and against, reform seek to show that it is on their side. During the decades of Direct Rule, the Westminster government resisted calls to legislate for abortion, referring to lack of support for change within NI. The local political environment was hostile to change with no prospect of reform from within the NI Assembly and political resistance to Westminster intervention. In 2008 leaders of all four main political parties in the NI Executive wrote to every MP expressing their opposition to abortion, claiming to represent the views of the overwhelming majority of local people (Horgan and O'Connor, 2014). This was a frequently cited response when the question of abortion reform was raised and it has been common for NI's 'distinctive cultural values' and in particular the cross community nature of public opposition to be cited as an obstacle to reform (O'Rourke, 2016).

Changing events, changing views?

There have been seismic political shifts in NI of late in relation to abortion. Between 2012 and the introduction of Westminster legislation decriminalising abortion in NI in October 2019, the issue of abortion attained a very high profile. A number of legal cases, an Optional Protocol Inquiry into abortion in NI by the UN CEDAW Committee (2018), an inquiry by the Women and Equalities Committee at Westminster (2019) and much increased NGO activity attracted considerable media interest (see Chapter Five). The case of Sarah Ewart and the legal action linked to it is seen as a watershed in the public debate on abortion in Northern Ireland and as having significant influence on political and public opinion. In 2013, Ewart spoke publicly of the traumatic impact of being forced to travel to access an abortion following a medical diagnosis of a fatal fetal impairment. This was covered extensively in the media as were the legal cases taken by the Northern Ireland Human Rights Commission and by Sarah Ewart herself. As discussed in Chapter Five, prosecutions of women buying abortion pills illegally on the internet were controversial and generated debate about the criminalisation of abortion.

Is there, however, robust evidence of the public opposition to reform frequently cited by politicians? Until the Northern Ireland Life and Times Survey in 2016 (NILT, 2016) fielded a module of questions on abortion there was no rigorous large-scale survey in NI. A small number of questions about abortion had been included in the Northern Ireland Social Attitudes (NISA) Survey in 1990. This showed that respondents favoured legal abortion in the case of three scenarios put to them: where the woman's health is seriously endangered by the pregnancy; where a woman is pregnant as a result of rape; and where there is a 'strong chance of a defect in the baby' (NISA, 1990).

Polls conducted in 2012 and 2014 by Lucid Talk for the *Belfast Telegraph* (Clarke, 2012; 2014) and by Amnesty International (2014) for the Family Planning Association showed a majority favoured legal abortion in some circumstances. The scenarios posed by each poll were different, making assessment of change difficult. The *Belfast Telegraph* polls appear to show a very significant increase (from 26 per cent to 58 per cent) between 2012 and 2014 in the number of respondents in favour of the proposition 'abortion should be available to any woman who chooses it after being counselled on the available alternatives'. Millward Brown, by contrast, reported a smaller proportion (59 per cent) in favour of abortion when a pregnancy resulted from rape or incest than had been recorded in previous surveys. In 2014 and 2016 Millward Brown also conducted polls for Amnesty International as part of their Omnibus survey. By this stage Amnesty International was actively campaigning for legal abortion in cases of rape, incest and fetal abnormality. The findings of the Millward Brown polls were consistent with previous polls in showing support for legal abortion in cases of rape and incest but also indicated growing public support for legal abortion in the case of fatal fetal abnormality (Amnesty International, 2014; 2016).

In the contested area of abortion policy in NI, polling and survey data have been increasingly used to demonstrate public support for particular stances. Two internet polls (ComRes, 2018, Both Lives Matter, 2019) commissioned by the anti-abortion group 'Both Lives Matter' were specifically concerned about a Westminster proposal to legislate to decriminalise abortion in NI. Respondents in the 2018 poll conducted by ComRes were presented with the following statement:

> At present, the law means abortion in Northern Ireland is decided by Stormont and is lawful only when there is a risk to the mother's life or to the long term physical or mental health. Some English MPs say that the Westminster Parliament should decide what the law is in NI and make it available for any reason up to 24 weeks in pregnancy. Do you agree or disagree with each of these statements on this issue:
>
> Changing the law on this issue should be a decision for the people of NI and their elected representatives and not for MPs in other parts of the UK.

Sixty-four per cent agreed with the statement; 23 per cent disagreed and 11 per cent said they did not know. The second internet poll, commissioned in October 2019, was carried out by Lucid Talk and asked respondents: 'Do you support the changes voted for at Westminster that will impose a new abortion regime in NI?'

Fifty-two per cent of respondents said they were opposed to the reforms and 39 per cent said they were in favour. Across every age group, opposition to the laws was stronger than support. The findings were argued by Both Lives Matter and others to indicate support for the status quo in NI. Most media coverage of the polls made no reference to previous attitudinal data or commented on the weighted language, for example, how phrases like 'some English MPs', or 'impose a new abortion regime' could influence responses. Nor did the media note the broader context of parliamentary debates. With no questioning of the validity of the poll, the results were cited during the Women and Equalities Select Committee inquiry into abortion in NI (Women and Equalities Committee, 2019) and in parliamentary debates on the Northen Ireland (Executive Formation) Bill. For example, Lord Morrow (DUP) stated that a 'ComRes poll shows that 64 per cent of the people of Northern Ireland oppose Westminster legislation for Northern Ireland on this matter, rising to 66 per cent of women and 72 per cent of 18 to 32 year-olds. We also know that all the main denominations in Northern Ireland oppose any change in the law' (Morrow, 2019: col 65).

The Northern Ireland Life and Times Survey

The most extensive and independent survey of public attitudes to abortion is the Northern Ireland Life and Times Survey (NILT), an annual cross-sectional survey set up in 2016 using a methodology similar to of the BSA. A systematic random sample of addresses are selected from the Postcode Address File database of addresses. The survey is conducted face to face. The questions on abortion in 2016, asked of 1,208 adults, were specifically designed as one part of a larger ESRC-funded study on abortion in NI and the UK at Ulster University. The NILT data recorded the level of support for the legalisation of abortion in seven given scenarios.

The survey showed high levels of public support for abortion being legal for 'hard' reasons: exceeding or nearing four in five respondents were supportive where the life of a woman is at risk; where there is a serious threat to her mental or physical health in continuing the pregnancy; in cases of fatal or serious fetal abnormality; and in cases of rape or incest. There was less support for a woman wanting an abortion because she had become pregnant and did not want to have the child: while 34 per cent agreed that abortion should be legal in this circumstance, 60 per cent of people held the view that it should *not*. However, 63 per cent agreed that '[i]t is a woman's right to choose whether or not to have an abortion'. Only 19 per cent of people felt that abortion should definitely or probably be illegal if 'a doctor says that there is more risk to the life of a pregnant woman if she continues with a pregnancy than if she were to have an abortion'. This wording is based on Ground C of the 1967 Abortion Act, which states that abortion is legal if two doctors believe: 'that the continuance of the pregnancy would involve risk to the life of the pregnant woman, greater than if the pregnancy were terminated', and is the basis – as noted in other chapters – for 98 per cent of abortions carried out in England and Wales (DHSC, 2019a).

Again, no significant gender differences in attitudes are seen and, with regard to age, 25–34 year olds are most likely to think that abortion should be legal. Respondents who lean towards criminalisation of abortion are more likely to be supporters of the Democratic Unionist Party (DUP), less likely to have a degree and more likely to attend church at least once a month (Gray et al, 2018). As in the rest of the UK, attitudes are strongly linked to religious affiliation. Catholics are less accepting of abortion than Protestants, while the strongest support for legalisation is expressed by those of no religion. However, as is also the case in Britain, people with a religious affiliation have also become more accepting of abortion in some circumstances. In NI, this is particularly notable among Catholics. In 1990, only 28 per cent of Catholics thought that the law should allow abortion where there is a strong chance of a serious 'defect in the baby'; by 2016, the figure had risen to 72 per cent of Catholics.

Overall, the 2016 NILT data indicated little support for criminalisation and growing public support for reform. In 2016, 70 per cent agreed with the statement: '[a]bortion should be a matter for regulation and not criminal law' and by 2018 this had risen to 82 per cent. While 71 per cent of respondents in 2016 agreed that a woman should never go to prison for having an abortion, by 2018 this had increased to 89 per cent, a possible response to criminal prosecutions and pending court cases relating to the buying of pills on the internet. The number saying '[i]t is a woman's right to choose whether or not to have an abortion' increased from 63 per cent in 2016 to 71 per cent in 2018. In sum, in 2019, there is evidence that while public opinion is nuanced there is significant support for decriminalisation of abortion in NI.

Why have attitudes towards abortion become more liberal in the UK?

The increasing liberalism in relation to abortion is in line with that seen in relation to other areas of sexual behaviour, premarital sex and same sex marriage, for example. Given the close link between religion and attitudes towards abortion, the increasing secularisation of society may have contributed to a trend towards generally softer views. Many countries in the west have seen a decline in religious identity and an associated trend towards a more socially liberal culture. As would follow from this, attitudes towards abortion in Britain are generally in line with those of other European countries. Pew Research examine views on abortion in 27 of the 34 countries in Europe. Between two thirds and three quarters of those sampled in northern European countries maintain that abortion should be legal, the proportion falling in countries in southern Europe, where the Catholic faith is more prevalent (Pew Research, 2018). Even in the United States, where the current political climate is by no means favourable towards abortion, public opinion has remained relatively stable with a steady 60 to 70 per cent majority, according to which poll is referenced, saying abortion should be legal in most or all cases (Guskin and Clement, 2019). The relationship between social liberalism generally and more liberal attitudes towards abortion, however, is not entirely clear cut. A cross-national study found that Japanese women were more favourably inclined towards abortion than those in the US because of harsher public attitudes towards childbearing outside of marriage (Hertog and Iwasawa, 2011).

Reasons more specifically related to attitudes towards abortion may include changing perception of what is involved in the procedure. Percentage support for abortion falls dramatically with an increase in gestational age at which abortions are carried out and is in single figures for those conducted in the second and third trimesters (Gallup, 2019). The advent of medical abortion, involving the use of mifepristone and misoprostol which, as noted in Chapter Three, has dramatically increased the proportion of abortions carried out in the first trimester using medication, is also likely to have influenced public opinion.

Changing social needs may also have served to modify attitudes and may have encouraged a more pragmatic stance on abortion. While in the 1950s two thirds of women were married or engaged to the person they first had sex with, today this figure is less than 1 per cent of the population. Little more than half a century ago, the interval between becoming sexually active and having a child was, on average, only three or four years. Today, some 14 or 15 years elapse between sexual initiation and becoming a parent and 20 per cent of women remain childless throughout life. Since there is still no perfect method of contraception in terms of acceptability, effectiveness and safety, the increased leniency seen in public opinion may well reflect an inclination to accommodate human fallibility with regard to unintended conception.

What is captured in the greater acceptance of abortion may also reflect the wider zeitgeist. Over recent years, support among medical bodies and professional associations has grown for abortion to be removed from the criminal law and for services to be subject to the same regulation as other healthcare procedures. It is unclear whether a change in attitudes is a direct result of the policy change, or whether policy changes came at a moment of shifting attitudes, but there are certainly grounds for seeing a reciprocal relationship between the two.

Evidence that there may now be a mismatch between the current law and the views of the public comes not only from social research into public attitudes but also from the actions of women themselves. In a four-month period between 2016 and 2017, 519 women in Britain self-sourced abortion medication on line. One of the reasons that they gave was to avoid the stigma of abortion, no doubt heightened by its legal status. Laws relating to abortion are changing the world over, and becoming more liberal, as noted in Chapter Six. It will be interesting to see whether the trend towards increasingly liberal views continues in Britain, and whether legal and policy developments around access to abortions will have any effect on public attitudes in the UK.

Conclusion

There has been a clear shift in recent decades towards a relaxation of attitudes towards abortion. The findings from the BSA and from the NILT show a substantial majority in favour of further liberalisation in Britain and a strong majority in favour of liberalisation of the previous, criminal law in NI.

THREE

How would decriminalisation affect women's health?

Patricia A. Lohr, Jonathan Lord and Sam Rowlands

Introduction

According to the UN Special Rapporteur on the Right to Health, criminal abortion laws jeopardise people's health and lives, subjecting them to physical and mental pain and suffering. Decriminalisation of abortion is recommended to alleviate these harmful effects (Grover, 2011). Yet, it is claimed by some in Britain that decriminalisation of abortion would have a negative impact on women's health. Sometimes it is argued that abortion is detrimental to women's health and any relaxation of the law will result in more abortions and therefore greater harm. Alternatively, it is suggested that the current legal framework for abortion is necessary to ensure higher quality care in the shape of better counselling, better consent procedures, and greater contact with doctors. It is asserted that without legal controls imposed on abortion providers, sub-standard and exploitative services would flourish.

This chapter evaluates the evidence for the effect of abortion on women's physical and mental health and how these are affected by the current legal framework. It assesses the likely consequences of decriminalisation on women's wellbeing and considers how moving from a model of healthcare designed as a defence against prosecution to one regulated like any other healthcare service would affect abortion care.

The safety of abortion

Abortion and maternal mortality and morbidity

Prior to 1968, the criminalisation of abortion in Britain was associated with high maternal mortality and morbidity. Many women with unwanted pregnancies were forced into procuring unsafe abortions. In the pre-*Bourne* era of the early 1930s, before the law was clarified (see Chapters One and Five), there were more than 300 deaths attributed to abortion in England and Wales annually (Figure 3.1). The mortality rate in a series of London women who reached hospital – and of whom half admitted illegal induction of abortion – was 18

Figure 3.1: Number of deaths from abortion (all causes), England and Wales, 1931–1951

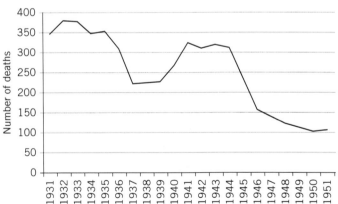

Source: The 20th Century Mortality Files 1901–2000, Office for National Statistics (ONS, 2011).

per 1,000 (Parish, 1935). The number of deaths attributed to abortion dropped annually in the late 1930s – followed by a setback during the Second World War – then falling to below 200 deaths after the war. Much of this improvement was due to advances in medicine, especially the development of antibiotics.

Morbidity from attempts to self-induce abortion included toxicity from chemicals or herbal extracts taken orally or applied locally and mechanical damage caused by sharp objects (Davis, 1950). Lead oxide was used in the 1890s and into the next century resulting in cases of lead poisoning with a fatal outcome in some instances (Hall and Ransom, 1906). Evidence submitted to the Birkett Committee in 1939 included cases of ingestion of ergot and quinine (Potts et al, 1977). Vaginal douching was carried out using caustic agents such as iodine, potassium permanganate, turpentine, carbolic soap or Lysol. Considerable injury was caused by the corrosive action of these agents (Davis, 1950). Many women visited illegal abortionists who used a wide variety of instruments: crochet hooks, umbrella ribs, hairpins, bicycle spokes, knitting needles, goose quills and meat skewers, to induce miscarriage (Potts et al, 1977). Slippery elm bark was also used as an osmotic cervical dilator which would then lead to the onset of labour and delivery (Parish, 1935). Objects such as rubber catheters were inserted into the uterus, or intrauterine injections of soapy water or Dettol were carried out with a Higginson syringe (Parish, 1935), the latter associated with air or fluid embolism. Later on, there was use of pennyroyal extract, sometimes with a fatal outcome (Vallance, 1955).

The advent of the Abortion Act in 1968 eventually led to an almost complete eradication of clandestine abortions with a further drop in deaths from abortion (Figure 3.2). Indeed, there are some years nowadays in which there are no deaths at all from abortion of any type in Britain. However, women still self-induce abortion, sometimes choosing an unsafe method. In 2010, Catherine Furey died from ingestion of industrial strength vinegar (Urquhart, 2014). These extreme measures

Figure 3.2: Trends in UK deaths from three categories of abortion before and after the Abortion Act came into force in 1968

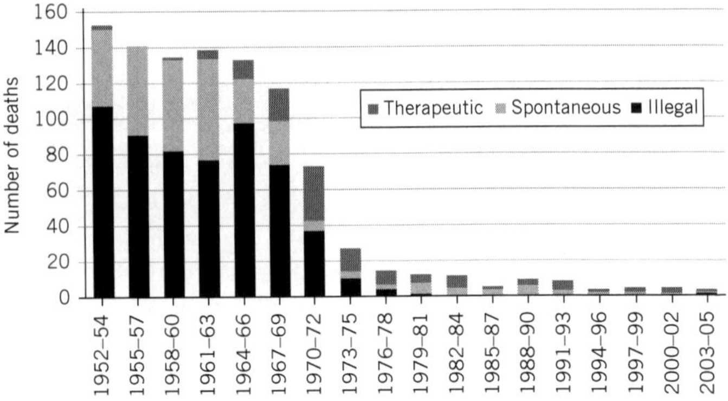

Source: Confidential Enquiries into Maternal Deaths (Lewis, 2007).

illustrate the desperation that women can feel about their unwanted pregnancies.

The risk of death from abortion is shown to be 32-times lower than that from childbirth when data from Mothers and Babies: Reducing Risk through Audits and Confidential Enquiries in the UK (MBRRACE-UK) 2003–2014 reports (NPEU, 2018) is combined with abortion statistics for England, Wales (DHSC, 2019a) and Scotland (ISD, 2019)(Figure 3.3). Maternal mortality for this period was 4.8 per 100,000 compared to abortion mortality of 0.15 per 100,000. To put these absolute levels of risk into perspective, the risk of dying in the UK over one year from a road traffic accident is 2.8 per 100,000 inhabitants (Department of Transport, 2018), of being murdered 1.2 per 100,000 (ONS, 2019b) and from all causes for women aged 25–29 is 0.3 per 100,000[1] (ONS, 2018). Morbidity from unsafe abortion also dropped immediately after the implementation of the Abortion Act. Hospital admissions for septic abortions fell from more than 2,000 cases a year in England and Wales to a negligible level (Potts et al, 1977).

The very low mortality associated with induced abortion has persisted with the development of new termination methods,

Figure 3.3: Comparison of maternal mortality and abortion mortality in Britain, 2003–2014 and other mortality comparisons, 2017/2018

Maternal mortality	Abortion mortality	Other mortality comparisons (UK data per 100,000 per year)	
• 9,126,256 maternities	• 2,501,348 abortions	Road traffic accident	2.8
• 434 direct deaths	• 4 deaths	Murder	1.2
• Rate 4.8 per 100,000	• Rate 0.15 per 100,000	All causes (age 25–29)	0.3

Source: MBRRACE-UK, Abortion Statistics for England and Wales, ISD and Office for National Statistics.

including the introduction of the abortifacient medication mifepristone in 1991. Mifepristone is used with a prostaglandin analogue such as misoprostol to induce abortion in a process similar to miscarriage. It is highly effective and avoids the need for surgery in almost all cases. It has been observed that the combination of mifepristone and misoprostol used in early pregnancy is a safer drug regimen than an injection of penicillin (Cates et al, 2003). The number of medical abortions has increased annually from 3,334 in 1992 to more than 150,000 in 2018 (DHSC, 2019a; ISD, 2019). During this period, the mortality rate for abortion was unchanged.

Abortion and longer-term health outcomes

Many conditions have been erroneously linked with abortion – those with the most media coverage being breast cancer and mental ill-health. There is solid evidence that no link between abortion and breast cancer exists, a position affirmed by many organisations including the Royal College of Obstetricians and Gynaecologists (RCOG), the National Institute for Health and Care Excellence (NICE), the National Cancer Institute (NCI), the American Cancer Society (ACS) and the American College of Obstetricians and Gynecologists (ACOG) (Rowlands, 2014). Authoritative reviews by the Academy of Medical Royal Colleges in the UK (AoMRC, 2011) and the American Psychological Association (Major et al, 2009) conclude that for women with an unwanted pregnancy, abortion does not harm their mental health. The relative risk of mental health problems among adult women who have a single, first-trimester abortion of an unwanted pregnancy in a safe environment is not greater than the risk among women who deliver an unwanted pregnancy. Danish registry studies have found that neither incidence rates of first psychiatric contact (Munk-Olsen et al, 2011) nor readmission rates (Munk-Olsen et al, 2012) for mental health disorders differ before and after abortion. In contrast, the same study found that rates of first contact with psychiatric services and readmission are increased within the first month after childbirth.

A number of studies have assessed subsequent reproductive outcomes after abortion (Rowlands, 2014). There is no association between abortion and infertility, ectopic pregnancy or placental abruption. There is some evidence for a protective effect of abortion on the development of pre-eclampsia, characterised by elevated blood pressure and high levels of protein in the urine, in future pregnancies (Trogstad et al, 2008). An association between surgical abortion and pre-term delivery has been noted in some studies but medical abortion does not appear to have the same association (Virk et al, 2007; Bhattacharya et al, 2012; Magro Malosso et al, 2018). Concluding a cause-and-effect relationship between abortion and any of these outcomes is problematic because they are population-based studies in which there is generally underreporting of abortion and they often do not include all of the factors that can influence pregnancy outcomes. For example, one study using data from over 1.3 million births derived from the Finnish Medical Birth Register found that smoking was the most significant risk factor for preterm birth (Räisänen et al, 2013). Past abortion, by itself, was not sufficiently important to be included in further modelling and analysis, being a lower risk than past miscarriage or use of in vitro fertilisation, or a similar risk to that of carrying a boy. Other reviews from smaller populations, such as a retrospective analysis from a Canadian obstetric unit (Hardy et al, 2013) and an earlier systematic review of 37 papers (Shah and Zao, 2009), reported a correlation between past abortion and preterm birth. However, no data were available for the systematic review to explore the effects of other risk factors such as smoking, and the Canadian paper noted that women who reported a prior induced abortion were in fact more likely to be smokers. Epidemiological evidence for an association between abortion and miscarriage or placenta praevia is also inconsistent and presents similar difficulties in determining causality. It is notable that these subsequent pregnancy outcomes have been found to be increased following caesarean delivery (Keag et al, 2018) suggesting that such risks are not always avoided, or may even be increased, by continuing a pregnancy.

There is also no evidence that having an abortion is detrimental to women's general physical health. A prospective cohort study reported that women who had had an abortion reported similar long-term physical health to those who gave birth (Ralph et al, 2019). When differences did emerge in that study, they were in the direction of worse health among those giving birth – women denied access to a wanted abortion reported worse long-term physical health than those who received an abortion.

The law versus best practice

The legalisation of abortion in Britain significantly reduced the risks associated with unsafe abortion. The vast majority of women are now able to access funded abortion care provided by skilled providers working in regulated environments (see Chapter Four). However, many of the requirements of the Abortion Act 1967 conflict with modern conceptions of healthcare and medical ethics, and interfere with the application of evidence to permit best practice, including the creation of a sustainable workforce. All this could not have been predicted but illustrates how out-dated the Act now is and the urgent need for change (Regan and Glasier, 2017). The sponsor of the Abortion Act, Lord David Steel, agrees that the Act is 'out of date' and 'badly in need of reform' and has called for decriminalisation (BBC, 2017).

Decision-making under the Abortion Act

Medicine has moved on substantially in the more than 50 years since the 1967 Act came into force. Paternalism in medicine is now viewed as inconsistent with accepted principles of medical ethics. Modern medicine respects people's autonomy, their ability to participate in shared decision-making and to freely make choices about their care (GMC, 2008; Beauchamp and Childress, 2013). Clinicians are advised to recognise the power differential in the medical model and not to abuse it or to project their beliefs and values onto their patients (Goodyear-Smith and Buetow, 2001). In other areas of medicine, the clinician advises a patient of options and the benefits and risks of each, empowering the patient to make an informed choice. This decision is then respected even if the clinician may not agree with it, as long as the patient has given consent that is informed, meaning the risk, benefits and alternatives are understood.

The requirement of the Abortion Act that it is only two doctors who can decide whether a woman meets the statutory grounds for abortion runs entirely against the principle that it is the patient's autonomy that is paramount. The stipulation for two doctors' approval, which protects the health professional against prosecution, is also medically unnecessary. It is entirely separate from the process of ensuring the woman has the information she needs to make a decision about treatment. Informed consent would remain essential after decriminalisation, while the current requirement to allocate a ground under the Abortion Act offers no benefit to the woman or to the safety of the process (Chapter Four).

Refusals of care on grounds of conscience can compromise access to abortion (Harries et al, 2014; Chavkin et al, 2017; Autorino et al, 2018) and can be harmful to health and wellbeing (Keogh et al, 2019). Regulations in some countries give priority to the rights of providers at the expense of women's timely access to abortion care. Currently in New Zealand, some healthcare providers object to making indirect referrals, thereby failing to ensure the safe transfer of a patient to the care of a colleague who does not have objections to abortion (Ballantyne et al, 2019). The General Medical Council states that personal beliefs must not be pursued where they are in conflict with the principles of good medical practice, treat patients unfairly, deny patients access to appropriate treatment or services, or cause distress to patients (GMC, 2013b). The extensive psychosocial and physical harms associated with denied abortion are well documented for women with an unwanted pregnancy, the child born subsequently and for existing children within the family (ANSIRH, 2019). Health service managers need to ensure that personal moralities do not interfere with service delivery. It has been argued that employment law deals better with this matter than healthcare law (Montgomery, 2015).

Some women may feel 'on their back foot' when requesting an abortion and that they need to justify their decision in some way. Having to create narratives which fit into the legal framework perpetuates the stigma associated with abortion (Purcell, 2015). This is not compatible with an open and honest discussion with a healthcare provider. When there are other issues which may be running alongside the abortion request such as reproductive control (Rowlands and Walker, 2019), this is not at all ideal. Neither is it necessary for the doctor to ask for and record reasons for an abortion. This reinforces the notion of 'good' and 'bad' abortions (Beynon-Jones, 2012; Bloomer et al, 2019). Decriminalisation would help to create a more 'open' and de-stigmatised atmosphere in consultations relating to abortion, which would have a beneficial effect on women's wellbeing.

Widespread concern was expressed to a parliamentary committee that the requirement for two doctors to attest that a woman meets at least one and the same ground under which a lawful abortion can be performed delays access to abortion (House of Commons Science and Technology Committee, 2007). Even though the absolute risk of mortality with abortion is now low, it increases as gestational age advances. One study estimated that if those who had abortions after eight weeks of gestation had been treated within the first eight weeks when risk is lowest, 87 per cent of abortion-related deaths likely could have been prevented (Bartlett et al, 2004). Complications associated with abortion, while also low, increase in number and severity when treatment is performed later in gestation. Certain medical conditions, such as heart disease, high blood pressure or kidney disease, can irreversibly worsen as pregnancy continues. In addition to affecting physical risks, women who have decided on a termination find it distressing to be kept waiting (Steinberg et al, 2016). They want their abortion procedure as soon as possible and identify minimal delay as a marker of a good service (Wiebe and Sandhu, 2008; McLemore et al, 2014; NICE, 2019). Delays may also restrict access to certain kinds of abortion methods, such as early medical abortion, which has an upper gestational age limit. Any healthcare professional would be concerned that delays to treatment may limit the available treatment options and cause unnecessary distress, but there is also a powerful economic argument. The National Institute for Health and Care Excellence (NICE, 2019) found that owing to the threshold effect of not being able to access medical abortion after an arbitrary legal limit, a reduction of one day in waiting time across the National Health Service (NHS) in England could save £1.6 million per year. A decrease of a week would save £11.5 million. Lastly, the requirement for two doctors' signatures creates a barrier to delivering responsive services. It either makes services unduly expensive; having doctors present merely to sign paperwork or, more likely – with a shortage of doctors wishing/willing to work in abortion care – women may have to return on another day. The Science and Technology Committee recommended that the requirement be removed (House of Commons Science and Technology Committee, 2007: para 99) and this would be achieved through decriminalisation.

Location of abortion

In the past, most abortions were performed in NHS hospitals. Now, in England and Wales, the majority are delivered under contract to the NHS from free-standing clinics run by independent-sector providers of abortion care, usually charities. In 2018, 72 per cent of abortions for residents in England and Wales were performed in the independent sector and 98 per cent were funded by the NHS (DHSC, 2019a). Like the NHS, these clinics are regulated by the Care Quality Commission (CQC) – or its equivalent in Wales and Scotland – with additional quality monitoring by Clinical Commissioning Groups and Health Boards to ensure timely access to services, adherence to national standards for healthcare service delivery, safety and national clinical guidelines (see Chapter Four). Clinics are staffed by a specialised workforce providing a bespoke service to ensure delivery of non-judgemental care within the gestational age limit permitted by law for treatment outside of hospital (23 weeks and 6 days) (Küng et al, 2018).

Delivery of abortion care outside of hospitals facilitates more care closer to home (Guthrie, 2010). Clinics are community-based, with some services being run by independent sector providers within general practitioner (GP) surgeries. It has also encouraged innovation and cost-effective, patient-centred approaches such as the use of local anaesthesia and moderate sedation rather than general anaesthesia for surgical abortion. These modalities can be provided in a treatment room as opposed to an operating theatre, thus needing less infrastructure and fewer staff. They also do not require the woman to starve before treatment, have faster recovery times, and may be associated with lower risks than general anaesthesia (RCOG, 2011). Such services have been early adopters of advances in other abortion technologies insofar as they have been able to do so within the strictures of the law.

The National Institute for Health and Care Excellence (NICE) recommends that abortion services are provided in a range of settings, including in the community (NICE, 2019). NICE conducted a systematic review that showed that there was a clinically important difference in patient satisfaction between community services and those delivered in hospital settings with community services rated higher than hospital settings (NICE, 2019a). They also found no evidence of inferiority for remote or telemedicine consultations. They concluded that community services and telemedicine appointments should be provided by the NHS because the evidence showed they both improve access to abortion services.

The Abortion Act was drafted when the only model for abortion care was a surgical procedure delivered in a hospital. Under the current regulations there is a complex process to gain approval as a place permitted to deliver abortion care where that place is not an NHS hospital. This makes development of better and novel models, such as delivery in primary care settings or by less intrusive methods such as through telemedicine, difficult. A statutory power, introduced in 1990, which permits the licensing of a 'class of places' for such purposes has, thus far, only been used in a limited way.

Abortion at home

Widespread legalisation and liberalisation of access to abortion in Europe and North America in the latter part of the twentieth century led to steep reductions in maternal mortality due to advances in abortion technologies as well as the establishment of safe, accessible services (Joffe, 2009). The latest technological advance in abortion care has been the introduction of simple and highly-effective regimens for the induction of abortion using pills. Medical abortion, with mifepristone and misoprostol, has transformed abortion care around the world. Introduced in Britain almost 30 years ago, medical abortion now accounts for 71 per cent of all abortions performed in England and Wales and 83 per cent of abortions at ten weeks of gestation or less (DHSC, 2019a). The rise in early medical abortions has been associated with a coincident increase in the number of abortions performed in the first trimester, when procedures are safest (DHSC, 2019a).

The Abortion Act 1967 permits the performance of abortions only within NHS hospitals or places approved by the Secretary of State for Health. Until recently, this meant that women in Britain could not realise the benefits of using misoprostol at home, a model of care demonstrated in comparative studies to be as safe, effective and acceptable as use within a clinical facility (Bar Ngo et al, 2011. Women's preference for home administration is easy to understand: it allows for greater privacy, better control over timing and better emotional support from those chosen by the woman while also reducing the burden on healthcare facilities (Lord et al, 2018). Prior to the approval of 'home' as a class of place where abortion can be performed, women were required to return to a clinical facility for administration of misoprostol after which they could be discharged to complete the abortion at home. Aside from creating logistical and financial barriers for women who were required to make more than one visit to a clinical facility for treatment, women suffered the discomfort of developing the effects of misoprostol – pain, bleeding and other side effects such as nausea and vomiting – as well as anxiety about passing the pregnancy on the way home (Lohr et al, 2010; Purcell et al, 2017). Where this happens it can be a very distressing experience, and is particularly significant for those reliant on public transport or who live in rural areas (Heller et al, 2016).

The interpretation of what is a permissible 'class of place' by the three respective government departments in Britain remains restrictive. Although England, Scotland and Wales all now permit the use of misoprostol outside of a clinic facility, there are limitations on the upper gestational age for its use in England (69 days of gestation) and in all three countries as to what constitutes the definition of 'home'. There is good evidence that outcomes at 64–70 days of gestation on the day of mifepristone administration are not different from 57–63 days of gestation (Winikoff et al, 2012; Bracken et al, 2014; Sanhueza Smith et al, 2015), and there is emerging evidence that with more than one dose of misoprostol, the upper limit could be extended further. Yet women at exactly 70 days of gestation must return to a clinical facility to receive misoprostol followed by discharge, incurring all of the previously mentioned disadvantages of this model of care. This group are also the most likely to benefit from additional doses of misoprostol to reduce the likelihood of complications such as incomplete abortion, but while extra doses can be supplied to women under 70 days of gestation for use at home, it would be illegal to provide them beyond this. In addition, despite mounting evidence that the administration of mifepristone is also as safely and as effectively used by women at home, and that they prefer it in many cases to use in a clinical facility, the limited approval of 'home use' to misoprostol precludes this advance in practice (Swica et al, 2013; Gold and Chong, 2015).

The restrictive definition of home as 'usual place of residence' (DHSC, 2018b) means that some women who ought to be offered the choice of medical abortion at home are denied it or are forced to return to a less appropriate environment to comply with the law. Examples of the detrimental effects of this constraint could include:

- women who would prefer to stay with a responsible adult at that adult's home (for example, a student with her parents or other safe, temporary accommodation);
- women who are in a place of safety that is not their normal home (for example, to avoid intimate partner violence);
- women who live in remote locations (for example, islands off the British mainland) where it would be safer for them to have treatment elsewhere (for example, on the mainland in a trusted friend's or relative's home);
- young women who, for example, live with their partner's parents but would rather be cared for by their own family;
- a minor in the care of separated parents, or other relatives;
- a minor in foster care, or in local authority accommodation;
- 'deemed ordinary residence' under the Care Act 2014: where a woman who is placed 'out of area' she is deemed to remain ordinarily resident in the area of the placing authority. This is the case for individuals in care home accommodation, in the 'shared lives scheme' accommodation, and in supported living accommodation;
- 'deemed ordinary residence' under the Mental Health Act 1983;
- non-EEA nationals without indefinite leave to remain; and
- anyone residing anywhere unlawfully.

Lastly, this persistent restriction on the location of use of abortifacient medications in early pregnancy means that services cannot develop innovative, cost-effective and desirable models of telemedical abortion care, including direct-to-patient provision of medications which could overcome geographical and other barriers. Examples of barriers that have been reported as reasons for women in England seeking to obtain abortion pills illegally online include being in a controlling or abusive relationship, work or childcare commitments, and perceived stigma (Aiken et al, 2018). No move has been made to license a broader 'class of places' in order to permit abortions to be offered in primary care, which is the preferred model in the newly established abortion service in the Republic of Ireland.

Expanding the provider pool

Task shifting/sharing is supported by the World Health Organization because it optimises the roles of healthcare workers (WHO, 2012b). Few abortions need to be provided by gynaecologists. General practitioners can safely and effectively play a major role in service delivery (Dressler et al, 2013; Gaudu et al, 2013; Dawson et al, 2017). Nurses, midwives and physician–assistants have all been found in clinical studies to be able to provide both early medical and early surgical abortion with similar outcomes to doctors (Gemzell-Danielsson and Kopp Kallner, 2014; Barnard et al, 2015). In South Africa and Vietnam, provision of surgical abortion by classes of healthcare provider other than doctors was shown to be highly acceptable (Warriner et al, 2006). In a Swedish study, medical abortion provided by midwives was shown to be as effective and safe as that provided by a physician (Kopp Kallner et al, 2015). In this study, although a majority of women were indifferent as to who provided the service, those who expressed a preference chose midwives to a larger extent. Pharmacists and pharmacy workers can also safely provide medical abortion (Tamang et al, 2018). There is good evidence that women prefer nurse- or midwife-led services over doctor-led services and that that there is a shorter time between referral and assessment in nurse-led services (NICE, 2019). NICE (2019) recommends that 'abortion providers should maximise the role of nurses and midwives in providing care'.

Decriminalisation, and the consequent removal of the requirement that an abortion must be performed by a registered medical practitioner, would allow use of much better staffing configurations, which would avoid current delays and increase patient satisfaction. In a recent study in Scotland on improvements that could be made to abortion services, the most commonly chosen response was the option to obtain an early medical abortion from a general practitioner (Smith and Cameron, 2019). General practitioners have formed an important part of the provider workforce in Canada and Australia, countries in which decriminalisation has taken place. They are also the primary providers of early medical abortion in Ireland, where abortion has recently been legalised. Alternatively, a wider range of health professionals working in sexual and reproductive health services could be used more for the delivery of abortion care. Unfortunately, the Abortion Act restricts both the scope of where services can be delivered and of who can deliver them. Therefore, while NICE, the organisation that appraises evidence and advises the NHS on best practice, recommends reform the current law will prevent this being put into practice.

Self-managed abortion

Decriminalisation allows further development of person-centred abortion practices. This includes self-care where women will not necessarily have direct contact with healthcare services. This is in line with current thinking at the World Health Organization (WHO, 2019), the general principles of self-care (Narasimhan et al, 2019), and the experiences and perceptions of women who have undertaken self-management of medical abortion (Wainwright et al, 2016). It has been shown that self-managed early medical abortion is mostly equivalent to that which is medically supervised, in terms of success rates and safety outcomes. Surgical evacuation rates may be higher (Endler et al, 2019b) due to aftercare provision by clinicians with little experience in settings in which abortion is legally restricted (Grossman, 2019). As is discussed in detail in Chapter Four, removal of criminal prohibitions against abortion would not compromise patient safety, with current regulations regarding the safe provision of medications that women may use on their own continuing to apply.

Medical abortion delivered with the use of telehealth has been shown to be as effective and safe as in-clinic provision and has a high satisfaction rating (Hyland et al, 2018; Gill and Norman, 2018; Endler et al, 2019a; Kohn et al, 2019). A recent prospective evaluation of a direct-to-patient model in the United States (Raymond et al, 2019) found that all 248 who were sent medications met eligibility criteria, all received the packages of medications sent to them, and no one took the medications at a gestational age where it would have been unsafe. Of those who had follow-up (n=217), 1 per cent (n=2) had a serious adverse event. One was hospitalised because of a seizure after an aspiration performed for bleeding. The second was hospitalised because of severe anaemia; she was diagnosed with complete abortion but received a transfusion. The authors determined that neither event would have been averted had the abortion medications been provided from a clinic setting.

Conclusion

The current general regulatory framework for healthcare, including abortion services, protects patients from harm and ensures high clinical and ethical standards (see Chapter Four). In contrast, the specific additional requirements imposed by the current legal framework for abortion services are cumbersome, bureaucratic and restrictive; they interfere with women's bodily autonomy, include unnecessary restrictions on where abortions take place and by whom they can be performed, and delay treatment which increases risk. Decriminalisation means that a woman can make her own decision about a pregnancy in light of the proven higher risk of mortality and morbidity of continuing the pregnancy (McGee et al, 2018), but would also have many other advantages over the *status quo*. Decriminalisation gives women the freedom to seek and undergo abortion without the 'chilling' effect of a possible custodial sentence. Abortion has an excellent safety track record; this applies to immediate complications and to longer-term effects. The safety of abortion is attributable to advances in medicine and regulation, not the threat of criminal prosecution, meaning that there is no reason to conclude that decriminalisation would harm women (see further Chapter Six). Abortions within the health sector, both medical and surgical, can be safely provided by a wide range of clinicians including gynaecologists, general practitioners, nurses, midwives and physician–assistants. Pharmacists can safely provide medical abortion. Self-managed abortion with access to medical back-up has similar success rates and safety outcomes to abortion that is medically supervised. Releasing the constraints on clinician groups and models of care would increase sustainability of abortion services and improve them by enhancing access, particularly at the earliest gestational ages when abortion is safest, and meeting women's needs and preferences.

Decriminalisation can be viewed as the foundation stone on which is built a health system with women's wellbeing and

Figure 3.4: Extract from joint statement by 12 organisations, including three Royal Colleges, in their briefing to the House of Lords, July 2019

Our position on abortion

We support the decriminalisation of abortion across the UK, including Northern Ireland. We believe that abortion should be treated and regulated like any other medical procedure – ensuring that women can access care locally and that healthcare professionals can provide the best services for their patients without the threat of prosecution.

Joint signatories

Alliance for Choice • Amnesty International UK • British Pregnancy Advisory Service (bpas) • British Society of Abortion Care Providers (BSACP) • Doctors for Choice (UK) • Faculty of Sexual and Reproductive Health • Liberty • Marie Stopes UK • Royal College of General Practitioners • Royal College of Midwives • Royal College of Obstetricians and Gynaecologists • Society of Radiographers

Source: https://bsacp.org.uk/wp-content/uploads/2019/08/Joint-briefing-Reform-of-abortion-in-Northern-Ireland.pdf.

rights as central tenets. There is growing professional support for decriminalisation of abortion in the UK (Regan and Glasier, 2017): it is now endorsed by several Royal Colleges and by the British Society of Abortion Care Providers (Figure 3.4).

In addition to eliminating harsh and unnecessary punishments on women (Bloomer et al, 2019) and those who provide safe abortion care, decriminalisation will ensure that the principles of choice and informed consent in healthcare decisions, now embedded in modern medical practice, apply equally to women's reproductive health and allow for advancements in abortion technologies and service delivery models to optimise abortion care.

FOUR

Would decriminalisation mean deregulation?

Jonathan Herring, Emily Jackson and Sally Sheldon

Introduction

Current British abortion law combines criminal prohibitions against abortion with an exception, carved out by the Abortion Act 1967, which provides that these offences do not apply where an abortion is performed in line with its requirements (see Chapter One). In the event of decriminalisation, the Abortion Act would necessarily be either very radically revised or repealed in its entirety alongside the removal of the criminal prohibitions. This has led some to worry that important safeguards against unethical or unsafe practice would be lost (for example, Caulfield, 2017: cols 30–1). In this chapter, we consider the basis for such concerns in the light of the legal regulation that would continue to apply following decriminalisation. We concentrate on the law of England, Wales and Scotland. Northern Ireland, where the Abortion Act has never applied, will be considered separately in the following chapter.

As we will show, the concern that decriminalisation amounts to deregulation is misplaced. Rather, abortion services are already (and would remain) subject to a dense web of other regulation, including general provisions of criminal and civil law, licensing and inspection requirements, and professional oversight (see further BMA, 2019). We begin by setting out the regulatory framework that is designed to promote good governance and high quality, patient-centred care in health services. We then move on to focus, in particular, on two issues that have provoked concern in the context of abortion services. First, we explain how the robust regulation of informed consent, confidentiality, counselling and safeguarding would be ensured following decriminalisation. Second, with a large majority of abortions now performed using medicines, we outline how access to abortion pills would be controlled. Finally, we turn to two specific cases that fall outside mainstream health practice: where a woman loses a desired pregnancy due to an assault or the non-consensual administration of pills; and where a backstreet abortion is performed by a professionally unqualified abortionist. Here, we suggest, where criminal sanction may remain appropriate, specific abortion offences are unnecessary as existing general principles of criminal law are sufficient to support prosecutions of morally culpable or dangerous conduct.

A general regulatory framework for safe care

It is rare to enshrine in statute law – as was done in the Abortion Act 1967 – restrictions on where, how and by whom a specific medical procedure can be authorised and performed. However, this does not mean that other modern medicine is practised within a legal vacuum. Rather, healthcare services are subject to significant and detailed regulation – including general requirements of civil and criminal law, licensing requirements and professional norms backed by disciplinary sanction – which foregrounds a concern with ensuring patient safety and promoting best practice. Abortion services are already subject to the requirements of this general framework and would remain so following decriminalisation.

First, it is a criminal offence to conduct any 'regulated activity' involving the provision of health or social care – including abortion services – without first being registered for this purpose. The relevant law differs slightly in its detail between England, Wales and Scotland. However, in each jurisdiction, registration depends on meeting detailed safety, quality and governance standards, with ongoing compliance monitored through inspection visits. In England, for example, providers of a regulated activity are subject to the detailed requirements laid down in the Care Quality Commission (Registration) Regulations 2009 and the Health and Social Care Act 2008 (Regulated Activities) Regulations 2014. These provide that service users must be treated with dignity and respect and safeguarded from abuse and improper treatment; that care and treatment must be provided in a safe way, with adequate staffing and good governance demonstrated; and that all equipment and premises must be properly maintained and suitable. In addition to these general requirements, which apply to all regulated services, this framework also offers a more flexible and easily updated mechanism for the imposition of requirements on specific areas of practice. For example, non-NHS abortion service providers are required to meet specified standards with regard to record keeping and the treatment of fetal tissue under the Care Quality Commission (Registration) Regulations 2009.[1]

Compliance with these requirements is overseen by the Care Quality Commission (CQC), which has a duty to inspect service providers under the Health and Social Care Act 2008. Where an abortion service provider falls below any of the standards set out in regulation, the CQC can serve improvement notices, cancel or alter a service provider's registration, and – in the most serious cases – bring prosecutions. Similar licensing, inspection and enforcement mechanisms operate in Wales, overseen by the Healthcare Inspectorate Wales (Care Standards

Act 2000; Registration of Social Care and Independent Health Care (Wales) Regulations 2002; Independent Health Care (Wales) Regulations 2011), and in Scotland by Health Improvement Scotland (NHS (Scotland) Act 1978; Healthcare Improvement Scotland (Requirements as to Independent Health Care Services) Regulations 2011).

Second, professional bodies exercise significant oversight over healthcare practice. Doctors are regulated by the General Medical Council, which operates with the overriding function of protecting, promoting and maintaining the health and safety of the public (Medical Act 1983). The General Medical Council issues a range of general guidelines that have relevance to abortion care (for example, GMC, 2007; 2008; 2012; 2013a; 2013b). Where the conduct of a doctor is found to pose a risk to the safety of patients or public confidence in doctors, the General Medical Council can suspend a doctor's right to work, require him or her to work under supervision or to undergo further training, or withdraw his or her licence to practice medicine. Likewise, the Nursing and Midwifery Council exercises oversight over nurses, midwives and nursing associates, who are required – again at risk of losing their right to practice – to act in accordance with the requirements to prioritise people, to practise effectively, to preserve safety, and to promote professionalism and trust (NMC, 2018).

Abortion service providers are also required to follow the detailed guidance offered by expert and professional bodies (or to offer a compelling explanation for any departure from it). The providers of a regulated activity are required to take account of any nationally recognised guidance relating to the services that they deliver (Regulation 12, Health and Social Care Act 2008 (Regulated Activities) Regulations 2014). Likewise, the General Medical Council expects doctors to demonstrate the maintenance of their skills, requiring an awareness of, and an adherence to, professional guidelines (GMC, 2013a). These two mechanisms give regulatory teeth to the detailed and comprehensive best practice guidelines on the organisation of abortion services, different abortion methods, and information to be given to patients produced by the Royal College of Obstetricians and Gynaecologists (RCOG, 2011b) and the National Institute for Health and Care Excellence (NICE, 2019), along with any guidance regarding specific aspects of services (for example, RCOG, 2010a; 2010b).

Third, it is important that women accessing abortion services are protected by the same principles of civil and criminal law that apply in the context of any other health service, since no regulatory framework, however robust, has ever succeeded in fully avoiding human error. Notably, all health professionals owe a duty of care to their patients and, where they fall below the standard of care that might reasonably be expected and a patient suffers harm as a result, they can be sued in negligence (*Bolam* 1957; *Bolitho* 1998). In the most serious cases, there may also be the possibility of a criminal prosecution for wilful neglect (sections 20–21, Criminal Justice and Courts Act 2015); for health and safety offences (section 7, Health and Safety at Work Act 1974); or for gross negligence manslaughter (*R v Adomako* 1994; *R v Misra* 2004). Those accessing NHS abortion services also have recourse to the general NHS complaints system.

Currently, independent sector abortion service providers are also subject to a separate approval process under section 1(3) of the Abortion Act 1967 that significantly predates, and today operates in parallel with, the general registration process for those offering a 'regulated activity'. This further approval process requires that service providers demonstrate their adherence to the terms of the Abortion Act; to the general requirements imposed on those who offer 'regulated activities'; and to the Department of Health's *Required Standard Operating Procedures* (RSOPs) (DH, 2014). If abortion were to be decriminalised, this additional approval process would likely disappear along with the other restrictions enshrined in the Abortion Act. While this would have the welcome consequence of sweeping away the unnecessary bureaucracy of two parallel approval processes, there is no reason to anticipate that it would compromise important safeguards regarding patient safety. On the contrary, scrutiny of the RSOPs – the large part of which is devoted to listing regulatory requirements that have independent force – illustrates the extent to which the legal framework for ensuring high quality abortion care is already to be found in general provisions of law and not in the specific framework governing abortion. As explained in this chapter, these provisions would continue to apply following any process of decriminalisation.

Informed consent, counselling, confidentiality and safeguarding

While it is important to make robust provision within abortion services for informed consent, confidentiality, safeguarding and access to counselling for those women who want it, the current criminal law framework plays no role in this regard. When two doctors certify that they believe, in good faith, that a woman's circumstances fit within one of the statutory grounds in the Abortion Act 1967, they are not playing any role in ensuring that the woman has voluntarily given informed consent to the termination. Or, if woman lacks capacity, it is not the Abortion Act which charges doctors with ensuring that a termination is carried out only if it would be in her best interests. If abortion were to be decriminalised, other mechanisms would continue to be in place to ensure that women voluntarily give informed consent to termination, and that the best interests of women who lack capacity are protected. Similarly, the confidentiality of a patient's abortion records is not protected by the Abortion Act, but by the rules which apply to all other sensitive information about a patient's medical treatment.

Informed consent and safeguarding

To carry out any medical procedure which involves touching, without the patient's informed consent, is a battery and an assault. Consent will be valid if it is given voluntarily, by someone who has the capacity to consent, and who understands, in broad terms, what the treatment involves. Hence, even if abortion is taken out of the criminal law, if a termination is carried out on a woman who has not voluntarily consented to it, she would not only have a civil claim in battery and in negligence, but also the person who carried out the termination would be likely to face a criminal charge of assault.

If a doctor were to suspect that a woman seeking an abortion was being pressurised by her partner or another family member, and that she did not, in fact, wish to terminate her pregnancy, he or she could not be confident that the woman had given a valid consent to termination. Doctors cannot rely upon a consent which has not been given voluntarily. So if a doctor were to terminate a pregnancy when he or she knows, or ought to have known, that the woman was not freely consenting to it, then he or she might be found to have committed both the tort of battery and the crime of assault.

Under the Health and Social Care Act 2008 (Regulated Activities) Regulations 2010, regulation 18, the registered person must have suitable arrangements in place for obtaining, and acting in accordance with, the consent of service users in relation to the care and treatment provided for them. In addition to these legal requirements to ensure that the person receiving medical treatment has consented to it, the CQC's Inspection Framework for Termination of Pregnancy (CQC, 2018) further requires providers to demonstrate that they ensure that women attending for abortion are certain of their decision, understand its implications and are seeking abortion voluntarily. If the pregnant woman does not speak English, relying upon her partner or another family member to translate for her is not good practice, and the CQC's framework prompts inspectors to ask whether in 'areas where ethnic minority groups form a significant proportion of the local population, are processes in place to aide translation during the consent process?'

Providers are likewise required to demonstrate that clinicians who care for women requesting abortion 'should be able to identify those who require more support than can be provided in the routine abortion service setting, for example young women, those with a pre-existing mental health condition, those who are subject to sexual violence or poor social support, or where there is evidence of coercion' (CQC, 2018; see further, RCOG, 2011b).

In addition to these abortion-specific requirements, doctors' ordinary responsibilities for safeguarding vulnerable adults and children would continue to apply after decriminalisation. If a doctor suspects that a child or an adult who lacks capacity is subject to abuse or neglect, he or she has a duty to inform the appropriate agency. For adults who have capacity, the duty is to work with the patient in order to help him or her to seek appropriate help, although in exceptional circumstances, where there is clear evidence of an imminent risk of serious harm to the individual, it can be appropriate to disclose information without her consent (RCPCH, 2014; HM Government, 2018).

Doctors' responsibility for obtaining informed consent from their patients is increasingly regarded as an aspect of the partnership model of medical decision-making, whereby both the doctor and the patient have expertise to bring to a decision about what medical treatment is appropriate (GMC, 2008; *Montgomery v Lanarkshire* 2015). Doctors have specialist skills in diagnosis and treatment, and they are sources of expert advice on the risks and benefits of different procedures, but the decision about what treatment is best for the individual patient, in the light of her priorities and interests, is ultimately one which the patient is uniquely well-placed to make for herself. For example, let us imagine that a serious fetal abnormality is detected at the 20-week anomaly scan. The doctor can advise the woman of the implications of that abnormality for a child's health and wellbeing but the pregnant woman knows better than the doctor how well she and her family would cope with the care of a child with that condition.

There is also a considerable body of good practice guidance which helps doctors to understand what the partnership model of medical decision-making involves. The General Medical Council's *Consent: Patients and Doctors Making Decisions Together* instructs doctors that, 'you must work in partnership with your patients to ensure good care', and that, in so doing, they must 'listen to patients and respect their views about their health', 'maximise patients' opportunities, and their ability, to make decisions for themselves', and 'respect patients' decisions' (GMC, 2008).

The partnership model also applies to abortion and doctors will discuss the risks, side-effects and implications of abortion with the pregnant woman, who will be able to weigh up whether termination is the best decision for her. However, in theory, this is superseded by the requirement under the Abortion Act that two doctors, rather than the woman herself, must determine whether termination poses less risk to her health than continuing the pregnancy. This is wholly at odds with modern medical practice. It casts an intimate medical decision as one which is *not* to be made by the patient herself, in the light of her own priorities and values, but as one that is to be made paternalistically, on her behalf, by two doctors.

Girls and women who lack capacity

The Abortion Act 1967 plays no role at all in protecting the interests of girls and women who lack capacity, whose interests are instead protected by the common law, by statute and by good practice guidance, all of which would continue to be in place if abortion were to be decriminalised.

Under 18s

If a girl is 16 or 17 years old, she is able to give a valid consent to termination, in the same way as if she were an adult (under the Family Law Reform Act 1969 in England

and Wales, and under the Age of Legal Capacity Act 1991 in Scotland). If she is under 16, but has sufficient understanding in order to make a decision for herself (*Gillick* 1986; Age of Legal Capacity Act 1991: section 2(4)), she can give a valid consent to abortion. She also has a right of confidentiality in relation to her termination, which means that her parents have no right to be consulted or informed (*Gillick* 1986; *Axon* 2006).

Parents can take medical decisions for children who are not yet *Gillick*-competent (England and Wales), or 'capable of understanding the nature and possible consequences of the procedure or treatment' (Scotland), subject to the possibility of being overruled by the court if the decision they wish to take is not in the child's best interests. In practice, however, the courts have been clear that it would be very difficult to imagine the circumstances in which it would be in the best interests of a girl who lacks capacity to terminate her pregnancy against her wishes, or, conversely, to force her to carry her unwanted pregnancy to term (*Re X (A Child)* 2014).

Adults who lack capacity

Where an adult pregnant woman lacks capacity, then under the Mental Capacity Act (MCA) 2005 in England and Wales and the Adults with Incapacity (Scotland) Act 2000, decisions about her pregnancy, including the decision to terminate it, should be made in her best interests (in the language of the MCA), or in order to benefit the woman (in the language of the Adults with Incapacity (Scotland) Act). Unlike non-therapeutic sterilisation, abortion is not one of the special cases for which court approval should be sought routinely. Rather, the decision should be brought before the Court of Protection in England and Wales or the Court of Session in Scotland only where there is doubt over whether the woman lacks capacity, or whether termination is in her best interests (*An NHS Trust v D* 2003; SCIE, 2011).

When deciding whether termination is in the best interests of a pregnant woman who lacks capacity, her wishes and feelings are of central importance (Adults with Incapacity (Scotland) 2000, section 1(4)(a); MCA 2005, section 4(6); *Re AB (Termination of Pregnancy)* 2019). That means that even if a woman would be unable to look after her baby, and the local authority would be likely to take the child into care immediately after birth, if a woman does not want a termination, it is very unlikely to be in her best interests (*Re AB (Termination of Pregnancy)* 2019). As King LJ has explained, 'carrying out a termination absent a woman's consent is a most profound invasion of her Article 8 rights' (*Re AB (Termination of Pregnancy)* 2019).

It is important to remember that – unlike any other medical procedure – where a decision is made by the woman's treating doctor, or by a court, that termination is in the woman's best interests, this is currently insufficient for the procedure to go ahead. Rather, in addition, the Abortion Act requires two doctors to certify that the woman's circumstances also fit within the statutory grounds. It could be argued that if the UK's capacity legislation is thought to offer sufficient protection to vulnerable women in the context of sterilisation, organ donation and the withdrawal of life-prolonging treatment, it is odd that a decision which has been taken in the woman's best interests (in England and Wales), or in order to benefit her (in Scotland), is not likewise the end of the matter in relation to termination.

Counselling

All women requesting an abortion should be offered the opportunity to discuss their options and choices with a trained counsellor, with this offer repeated at every stage of the care pathway and post-abortion counselling available for those women who request it. No provision for this is made in the Abortion Act. Rather, these requirements are enshrined in professional guidelines (RCOG, 2011b; NICE, 2019) and regulation (CQC, 2018). Following decriminalisation, provision for counselling would thus continue in exactly the same way as currently.

Confidentiality and data protection

Information about a woman's termination of pregnancy is undoubtedly sensitive personal information, and further disclosure of it is protected at common law, by her right to privacy under the Human Rights Act 1998, and by the General Data Protection Regulation 2018. Under the Abortion Regulations 1991, every abortion must be reported to the appropriate Chief Medical Officer, and the Regulations place restrictions upon any further disclosure of this information. If abortion were to be decriminalised, this is not a reason to stop collecting data about the incidence of abortion in England, Scotland and Wales, and similar reporting duties could be imposed through a new set of Regulations.

Regulation of abortion medicines

In 2018, 71 per cent of abortions performed in England and Wales and 86 per cent of those in Scotland were medical rather than surgical (DHSC, 2019a; ISD, 2019). Medical abortions involve the sequential administration of two prescription-only medicines, mifepristone and misoprostol, in order to end the pregnancy and trigger a miscarriage. If abortion were to be decriminalised, the law which applies to the provision of prescription-only medicines would continue to impose considerable restrictions upon the supply and use of mifepristone and misoprostol.

Medicines can only receive a marketing authorisation under the Human Medicines Regulations 2012 if they are proved to be safe and effective. The Human Medicines Regulations also ensure that medicines which are supplied for human use meet appropriate quality standards. Supplying counterfeit or fake medicines is a criminal offence under statute in England and Wales (section 2, Fraud Act 2006) and common law in Scotland.

Medicines are classified as 'prescription only' in order to ensure that only properly qualified and registered healthcare professionals act as gatekeepers to anyone wishing to access them. The General Medical Council's good practice guidance for doctors specifies that doctors must not prescribe any medicines unless they have 'adequate knowledge of the patient's health, and are satisfied that the drugs or treatment serve the patient's needs' (GMC, 2013a: para 16(a)).

It is a criminal offence for someone who is not properly qualified and registered to prescribe and supply a prescription-only medicine (regulation 214, Human Medicines Regulations 2012). Hence the owners of any 'online pharmacy', which claims to sell mifepristone and misoprostol without a prescription would be committing a criminal offence in the UK. In practice, such websites are often based overseas, and it is therefore more difficult for the UK regulator of medicines, the Medicines and Healthcare Products Regulatory Agency (MHRA) to control their activities. If the website is registered in another country, the MHRA would inform the relevant regulatory authority in that country.

There are also restrictions upon advertising. Prescription-only medicines cannot be directly marketed to consumers, and regulation 283 of the Human Medicines Regulations 2012 further provides that 'A person may not publish an advertisement that is likely to lead to the use of a medicinal product for the purpose of inducing an abortion'.

Non-consensual termination of pregnancy

The current law has little difficulty in dealing with cases where the defendant terminates, or seeks to terminate, the victim's pregnancy without her consent. Indeed, in recent years, in England and Wales, the primary use for the offences under section 58 of the Offences Against the Person Act 1861 and the Infant Life (Preservation) Act 1929 has been in cases where the defendant causes a woman (frequently his former or current sexual partner) to lose a wanted pregnancy. For example, in *R v Magira* 2008, a husband, who was unhappy about his wife's pregnancy, mixed abortion pills into her food without her knowledge, which made her ill, but did not cause a miscarriage. He was convicted of administering a poison or noxious thing with intent to secure a miscarriage under section 58 of the Offences Against the Person Act. He received three years and nine months' imprisonment.

Even if those offences were abolished, however, other offences are committed in such cases. The general offences of assault occasioning actual bodily harm (section 47, Offences Against the Person Act 1861) and causing/inflicting grievous bodily harm (sections 18 or 20, Offences Against the Person Act 1861) apply. Under the current law, grievous bodily harm has been defined as really serious bodily harm and it is left to the jury to determine if an injury falls within that description (*R v Bollom* 2003). It seems very likely that a jury would conclude that a non-consensual termination would constitute grievous bodily harm and, indeed, it seems in the reported cases that they have been willing to do so. In *R v Wilson* 2016, the defendant attacked the pregnant victim (his former sexual partner), deliberately stamping on her stomach. He was convicted of intentional infliction of grievous bodily harm (as well as 'child destruction' under the Infant Life (Preservation) Act 1929). Indeed, in such cases it can be easier to charge one of the general assault offences than to rely on section 58 of the Offences Against the Person Act or the Infant Life (Preservation) Act, because there is no need to prove that the defendant knew the victim was pregnant or that he was intending to terminate the pregnancy.

The poisoning offences found in sections 23 and 24 of the Offences Against the Person Act 1861 are also important here. Section 24 states that 'whosoever shall unlawfully and maliciously administer to or cause to be administered to or taken by any other person any poison or other destructive or noxious thing, with intent to injure, aggrieve, or annoy such person' is guilty of an offence. Section 23 is similarly worded but covers cases where the victim's life is endangered or they suffer grievous bodily harm. A very senior judge, Munby J (as he then was) seems to have accepted *obiter dicta* that these offences could be used to punish a defendant who had sought to terminate a victim's pregnancy without her consent through the surreptitious administration of pills (*R (Smeaton)* 2002: para 274).

There is, therefore, plenty of scope within the current criminal law to deal with cases where a defendant is seeking to terminate a victim's pregnancy without her consent. Indeed, we cannot imagine such a case where a criminal offence would not be committed, even if section 58 of the Offences Against the Person Act and the Infant Life (Preservation) Act were abolished. While it is thus highly unlikely that such an amendment is required, if Parliament deemed it desirable for the removal of any doubt, it might nonetheless choose to amend the existing offences to provide explicitly that the surreptitious administration of pills falls within the poisoning offences and that an assault on a pregnant woman that terminated a pregnancy would be treated in law as 'grievous bodily harm'. This latter proposal was made by the Victorian Law Reform Commission (VLRC, 2008: 8), which suggested accompanying decriminalisation of abortion with an amendment to the law criminalising the causing of serious injuries. This provided that '[s]erious injury includes: the destruction (other than in the course of a medical procedure) of the fetus of a pregnant woman, whether or not the woman suffers any other harm'.

Reform in relation to sentencing might also be considered, though again, in our view, this is not necessary as the matter is adequately dealt with by the current law. A defendant who attacked a pregnant woman, terminating her pregnancy, could be charged with the same offences under sections 23 or 24 as could a defendant who attacked a woman who was not pregnant. However, under the current law, the loss of a wanted pregnancy will be treated as an aggravating feature which would indicate an increased sentence. In *R v Wilson* 2016, an 18-year sentence was held to be justified, with the court placing particular weight on the intentional termination of the pregnancy through the attack. The maximum sentence for intentional infliction of grievous bodily harm is life and so this sentence could have been imposed even without a conviction under the 1929 Act.

Medically unqualified providers

It has been questioned whether, if the relevant offences under the Offences Against the Person Act and Infant Life (Preservation) Act (in England and Wales) and the common law (in Scotland) were abolished, it would then become lawful for someone who does not have the appropriate qualifications or training to provide an abortion (Caulfield, 2017 30–1). There are two main reasons why this should not be a concern.

First, it is an offence to falsely pretend to be a doctor, nurse, or midwife (section 49 of the Medical Act 1983; section 44 of the Nursing and Midwifery Order 2001; and, for England and Wales, section 2 Fraud Act 2006). That would clearly cover anyone who was purporting to be medically qualified at performing abortions, but in fact was not. It would not, however, apply to someone who was open about not having any medical qualifications.

Second, as confirmed in the infamous decision of the House of Lords in *R v Brown* 1993, any medical procedure that involves contact with the body of a patient is *prima facie* a criminal offence. It could be an assault occasioning actual bodily harm (section 47, Offences Against the Person Act) or inflicting/causing of grievous bodily harm (sections 18 and 20 Offences Against the Person Act), depending on the severity of the harm. However, for such offences, the consent of the patient only provides a defence in a list of exceptional circumstances, one of which is 'reasonable surgical interference'. The precise scope of this exception was considered by the Court of Appeal in *R v BM* 2018, which concerned a tattooist who had engaged in body modification (including ear removal and tongue splitting) on clients with their consent. When charged with offences of causing grievous bodily harm, he sought to rely on the medical treatment exception. The Court of Appeal rejected this defence, explaining it could not be used by people not qualified to practise surgery:

> elective surgery would only be reasonable if carried out by someone qualified to perform it. The professional and regulatory superstructure which governs how doctors and other medical professionals practice [sic] is there to protect the public. The protections provided to patients, some of which are referred to in the medical evidence before the judge, were not available to the appellant's customers or more widely to the customers of those who set themselves up as body modifiers. (para 42)

The Court of Appeal went on to explain that those lacking medical qualifications were not in a position to ensure that the patients had the capacity to make the decision to consent to the treatment, or had been properly informed of the risks. Notably, they explained that the fact the 'surgery' was performed with skill and in sterile conditions did not affect their decision. Nor was the fact the clients were willing to consent to the treatment, knowing the defendant was not medically qualified. This case makes it clear that a person who performs a surgical termination of pregnancy, which would otherwise be an assault occasioning actual bodily harm or grievous bodily harm will be guilty of an offence under the Offences Against the Person Act because they cannot rely on the medical treatment exception.

There is, perhaps, one issue of debate. It is only necessary to rely on the medical treatment exception if the treatment involves actual bodily harm or a more serious harm. While later abortions performed by dilatation and evacuation would certainly fall into that category it might be questioned whether earlier procedures performed by vacuum aspiration procedures would also do so. Actual bodily harm has been defined by the courts as any hurt which interferes with the health or comfort of the victim, which is more than transient and trifling (*R v Chan Fook* 1994). The approach taken by the House of Lords in *Brown* is that this is assessed without taking into account the consent of victim. Given the courts' emphasis on ensuring that medical procedures are offered by those trained to ensure informed consent, it seems likely that even a safely performed vacuum aspiration procedure would constitute a bodily interference which is more than transient and trifling. It should also be remembered that, as outlined earlier, abortion is a 'regulated activity', meaning that it is a criminal offence to offer services without first being registered to do so.

Conscientious objection

Finally, it should be noted that the Abortion Act also offers a safeguard designed to protect the interests of those healthcare professionals who are opposed to abortion for religious or moral reasons, providing that 'no person shall be under any duty ... to participate in any treatment authorised by this Act to which he has a conscientious objection' (section 4(1), Abortion Act 1967). If abortion were to be decriminalised, abortions would no longer be 'authorised by this Act' and statutory protection of conscientious objection rights would thereby disappear.

It is a moot point whether statutory protection of conscientious objection rights is necessary. Notably, the statutory right does not cover those doctors who choose to opt out of certifying that an abortion is justified under the Abortion Act, as certification must legally take place *before* treatment for the termination of pregnancy begins and thus cannot logically constitute 'participation in any treatment' (*Doogan* 2014: para 36; *Janaway* 1989: 572). Nonetheless, doctors' right to opt out of certification is widely respected in practice and is entrenched in employment law, the contractual arrangements made by the NHS with GPs and the employment contracts made with hospital doctors (*Doogan* 2014: para 36).

Whether or not to entrench a statutory right of conscientious objection post-decriminalisation would be a matter for Parliament. The Abortion Bill 2018, sponsored by Diana Johnson, made such provision.

Conclusion

If the specific criminal offences against abortion in England, Wales and Scotland were to be abolished, the Abortion Act would become redundant and should thus also be repealed. Such moves would necessarily be the result of statutory reform, allowing Parliament the opportunity to retain any provisions of the Act that it believes to serve an ongoing purpose. For example, Parliament might choose to make specific provision for conscientious objection. While in our view this is not necessary, Parliament might also amend existing assault and poisoning offences to put beyond any doubt that they apply to non-consensual abortion.

In other respects, as we have described earlier in the chapter, abortion is – and would remain – subject to a dense web of other regulation. It is these provisions which already do the important work of ensuring that services are of a high quality; and that they are offered with close attention to the need for robust consent, confidentiality, counselling and safeguarding. In rare cases – involving non-consensual or unsafe abortions offered by unqualified providers – criminal sanction would remain appropriate. As previously described, in our view, it is already so available under the general provisions of criminal law.

We have not sought to address moral, theological or political arguments regarding the decriminalisation of abortion. We have, however, demonstrated that any concern that abortion would be left unregulated following such a reform are ungrounded and should therefore not play a role in those debates.

In sum, decriminalisation does not amount to deregulation.

FIVE

The effects of decriminalisation in Northern Ireland

Marie Fox and Goretti Horgan

Introduction

In July 2019, the Westminster government voted to require the Secretary of State for Northern Ireland to give effect to the report of an influential Committee on the Elimination of Discrimination Against Women (CEDAW) Inquiry, which had found that Northern Irish law breached human rights norms (CEDAW, 2018). As this volume goes to press in late 2019, this radical change to Northern Ireland's abortion legislation has just come into effect, although details of the new governance regime that will follow have yet to be published. Until October 2019, Northern Ireland was governed by one of the most restrictive legal frameworks for abortion in the world and, as a result, only extremely limited abortion service provision currently exists. From midnight on 21 October 2019, the relevant provisions of the Offences Against the Person Act 1861 were repealed for Northern Ireland, with a moratorium introduced on criminal prosecutions. Effectively, this decriminalises most terminations in Northern Ireland,

and, somewhat ironically, places Northern Ireland in the vanguard of the movement to decriminalise abortion in the United Kingdom. However, even before this momentous change occurred, it was clear that Northern Irish women continued to access abortions and that the restrictive abortion governance regime was only sustainable due to the ability of some women – often at significant cost and under threat of prosecution – to travel to avail themselves of abortion care or to access abortion pills online.

This chapter will begin by outlining the law that obtained until October 2019, explaining the limited circumstances in which it was possible lawfully to end a pregnancy within Northern Ireland. It will then assess the adverse impact of criminalisation on women's health and welfare, drawing on a recent empirical study of the experience of Northern Irish women faced with unwanted pregnancies who were forced either to travel elsewhere for abortion or to use abortion pills outside of formal health services. The following section will outline how the courts and a range of international bodies found that the pre-reform position meant that the UK government breached its international human rights obligations. The chapter will conclude by outlining the clear infrastructure that exists for the provision of abortion services within Northern Ireland, which will be supplemented by measures to be put in place following a period of consultation. Consequently, repeal of the abortion provisions of the 1861 Act will not result in the regulatory vacuum some have predicted.

The legal position in Northern Ireland prior to October 2019

As noted in Chapter Four, the Abortion Act 1967 never extended to Northern Ireland, so the exemption for health professionals who perform terminations on grounds enshrined in that legislation never applied. Consequently, the legal position in Northern Ireland was governed by two very old statutes – the Offences Against the Person Act 1861 and the

Criminal Justice Act (Northern Ireland) 1945. As outlined in Chapter One, the 1861 Act created the criminal offences of 'unlawful procurement of miscarriage' (section 58) and of knowingly or intentionally 'supplying or procuring an instrument or poison or other noxious thing' in order to procure a miscarriage (section 59). Section 25 of the 1945 Act created a separate offence of intentionally destroying 'the life of a child capable of being born alive'. Effectively this provides an alternative charge where pregnancy has reached a gestation of 24 weeks or more. While the text of the 1945 Act (identical to the Infant Life (Preservation) Act 1929) explicitly refers to a presumption that 'evidence that a woman had at any material time been pregnant for a period of 28 weeks or more shall be prima facie proof' of viability, it is now widely accepted that a fetus will be viable at 24 weeks. In Great Britain, this understanding of viability was reflected in an amendment to the 1967 Abortion Act by the Human Fertilisation and Embryology Act 1990, enshrining a 24-week limit on the face of the Act for most abortions. In Northern Ireland guidance issued by the Department of Health in 2016 also clearly recognised that the point of viability had shifted since 1945 (DHSSPS, 2016: paras 2.11–12).

Post-viability, the 1945 Act provided a statutory defence where the act of child destruction was undertaken to 'preserv[e] the life of the mother', whereas the 1861 Act contained no such defence. It was therefore unclear, until the late twentieth century, whether a health professional in Northern Ireland who carried out a termination before the fetus was capable of being born alive had any defence to a charge of procuring a miscarriage. In a series of decisions in the mid-1990s the High Court in Belfast confirmed that the 1939 ruling in *R v Bourne* (which as a jury direction in a Crown Court trial was technically not binding in Northern Ireland) applied to terminations in Northern Ireland. However, judges interpreted the *Bourne* ruling extremely narrowly. In *Bourne,* McNaghten J had directed the jury that if the doctor's view was that the pregnancy would render the woman 'a physical or mental wreck', it was justifiable to perform an abortion. In the Northern Irish cases this so-called '*Bourne* exception' was restrictively construed. Most significantly, in *Re AMNH* (1994) it was held that continuation of the pregnancy must pose a 'real and serious risk' to the woman's health, while *Western Health and Social Services Board v CMB* (1995) emphasised that the risk must be 'permanent or long term'. More recently, the Northern Ireland Court of Appeal suggested that the test should be more widely interpreted so as to encompass the cases of the women and girls who gave evidence in a case brought by the Northern Ireland Human Rights Commission (*Re NIHRC* 2017; see p 90 in this book); however this did not result in any change to professional guidance.

In summary then, by mid-2019, and notwithstanding the suggestion of the Northern Irish Court of Appeal, abortion was only available if termination was necessary to preserve the life of the woman, or if continuing the pregnancy posed a risk of real and serious adverse effect on her physical or mental health, which would be long term or permanent (DHSSPS, 2016). Many women or girls who had become pregnant as a result of rape or incest did not readily fit within this interpretation. Those with wanted pregnancies who sought termination when their fetus was diagnosed with a fatal condition had to convince health professionals that the impact on their mental health was such that they came within this restrictive interpretation of *Bourne*. More generally, as is seen in the following section, the impact of the law was that all women and girls were at risk of being charged with serious criminal offences if they sought to end an unwanted pregnancy. As an influential Amnesty International Report in 2015 had summarised:

> For many women, demonstrating a long-term risk to health, particularly mental health, and overcoming barriers to access to abortion in Northern Ireland is often

an unsurmountable challenge. Women's access to and experience with health services also varies depending on the attitude of and availability of services within each of Northern Ireland's NHS health trusts … which leads to further inequity. (Amnesty International, 2015: 6)

The impact of criminalisation

Women or girls with unwanted pregnancies were thus forced either to travel to access abortion care elsewhere or to purchase abortion medication online. For decades no prosecutions had occurred under the 1861 Act, although a 1994 survey of GPs in Northern Ireland found that 11 per cent of them had seen the results of 'amateur attempts' at inducing abortion (Francome, 2004). However, following devolution in December 1999, the position changed. The Department of Health issued several iterations of Guidance on Termination of Pregnancy for health professionals, with the text finally agreed and published in 2016 (DHSSPS, 2016). Each version emphasised that the punishment for any doctor carrying out an illegal abortion was life imprisonment. The chilling effect of such Guidance meant that the number of reported legal abortions in Northern Ireland dropped from 80–100 a year pre-devolution to just 12–14 a year in 2016, 2017 and 2018 (DHSC, 2019a). A controversial circular sent in early 2013 by the Attorney General for Northern Ireland advising all obstetricians and gynaecologists that any failure to practise within the law risked prosecution and imprisonment compounded this chill factor (RCOG, 2018).

These low numbers did not signify that women were not having terminations; rather over 1,000 Northern Irish women travelled annually to England and Wales to access abortions. In 2018, 1,053 abortions were performed on women from Northern Ireland – an increase of 192 from 2017. This contrasts with a peak figure of women travelling of 1,855 in 1990 (DHSC, 2019a). Until 2017 not only did abortion-seeking women have to cover travel costs, but to fund the procedure themselves, typically spending upwards of £900 to access abortion. Even though such women were generally UK taxpayers, the policy requiring them to pay for abortions in Britain withstood legal challenge (*R (on the application of A and B) v Secretary of State for Health* 2017). As Lady Hale noted, in her dissenting judgment in the UK Supreme Court:

> The right of pregnant women to exercise autonomy in relation to treatment and care has been hard won but it has been won… This [decision] is to deny pregnant women from Northern Ireland the same right to choose what is done with their bodies as is enjoyed by all other pregnant citizens of the United Kingdom. It is inconsistent with the principle of equal treatment which underlies so much of our law. This is not to say that the law in Northern Ireland has to be the same as the law in the rest of the United Kingdom… But it is to say that a woman from Northern Ireland who is in Great Britain ought not to be denied, as a matter of policy, the same rights as other women here enjoy. (*R (on the application of A and B) v Secretary of State for Health* 2017: 93, 95)

In June 2017 Chancellor Phillip Hammond was forced to announce that the UK government would, via the Equalities Office, fund abortions for women ordinarily resident in Northern Ireland (Elcot and McDonald, 2017). This decision averted a potentially divisive vote on an amendment to the same effect to the Queen's Speech of 2017 proposed by Stella Creasy MP. The policy shift was followed by a marked increase in the numbers travelling for abortion, vividly illustrating the socio-economic barriers erected by the law. The volume of women travelling in quarters three and four of 2017 increased by 36 per cent and 58 per cent respectively compared to the same quarters in 2016 (DHSC, 2018a). Yet, notwithstanding this increase due to the new financial arrangements, obstacles to travel remained. In 2018 an All-Party Parliamentary Group highlighted the need for clear guidance on funding, and provision of a care pathway for women travelling from Northern Ireland (APPG, 2018: 38).

Furthermore, the CEDAW Inquiry report (2018) and the Women and Equalities Committee Inquiry report (2019) recognised that there will always exist those for whom travel is not an option. These include disabled women; women with caring responsibilities or in controlling relationships/family situations, or with visa issues; and women who are too poorly paid to afford to take a couple of days off work. Indeed, for some women even visiting a doctor may be difficult. More broadly, as the report concluded, travel can never be an optimal solution for any woman seeking termination, given the consequences for follow-up care and the emotional burden in a society that continues to stigmatise abortion.

Over the last decade, women have also been able to access abortion pills via one of a number of 'telemedicine' websites. The combination of abortion pills and the internet has transformed access to abortion, meaning that women in Ireland, North and South, can access abortion in their own homes (Aiken et al, 2017). Currently at least six websites provide telemedicine access, as well as information and support on using the pills safely (Jelinska and Yanow, 2018). Adverse incidents from the use of medical abortion are rare, although the websites advise women, where possible, to end their pregnancy within an hour's drive of a hospital in case of complications. In Northern Ireland the chances of women seeking such medical assistance were greatly reduced by a combination of section 5 of the Criminal Law Act 1967, which imposes a general obligation to report crimes, and the 2016 DHSSPS guidance, which required healthcare professionals to report a suspected illegal abortion. The Guidance states:

> the health and social care professional need not give that information if they have a reasonable excuse for not doing

so; the discharge of their professional duties in relation to patient confidentiality *may* amount to such a reasonable excuse. Professionals should be clear, however, that *patient confidentiality is not a bar to reporting offences to the police.* (DHSSPS, 2016: para 6.1, emphasis added)

While it elsewhere suggests a 'don't ask, don't tell' approach to women presenting at a hospital who may have induced the abortion (DHSSPS, 2016: para 6.3), this did little to allay the fears expressed by participants in the study outlined later in the chapter.

Such fears are well founded given the punitive approach the authorities have adopted for those obtaining abortion pills via the internet. For instance, in 2015, a woman was charged with obtaining pills for her 15-year-old daughter (Carroll, 2018) and in January 2016 a 21-year-old woman pleaded guilty to procuring an abortion using pills, receiving a suspended prison sentence (McDonald, 2016). Later in 2016 a couple accepted a police caution on the same charge; thereby admitting an offence which would remain on their record for at least six years. In March 2017, two activists' homes were raided by police with search warrants, looking for abortion pills. That same month, 15 to 20 women had their pills seized by customs; police officers visited most and requested they come to the station for questioning (Noble, 2017). The CEDAW report noted that the police have investigated over 30 cases of individuals suspected of procuring an abortion in Northern Ireland since 2000 and that between 2006 and 2015, the Police Service of Northern Ireland made 11 arrests related to illegal abortion. Between 2011 and 2016 five people were questioned and arrested for possession of abortifacients; two were convicted (Women and Equalities Committee, 2019: para 19). The woman prosecuted for obtaining abortion pills for her daughter sought a judicial review of the decision to prosecute. However, under the moratorium introduced by the 2019 legislation, the prosecution against her has been dropped, and consequently the review will not proceed. Nonetheless, these examples of women's lived experience of prosecution, or the threat thereof, counter any suggestion that the fear of prosecution is overstated. That impact is reinforced by the empirical study to which we now turn.

The research, funded under the ESRC's Transformative Research programme, explored public attitudes to abortion (see Chapter Two) and compared the experiences of women in Northern Ireland, who accessed abortion pills outside the law and the formal healthcare system, to those of women in Scotland, who accessed pills via the NHS (Horgan, 2019). While the core of the study was qualitative, comparing experiences of women in Northern Ireland to those of women in Scotland, the researchers also had access to a sample of 333 women living in Northern Ireland who accessed abortion pills from the feminist website Women Help Women, in 2016/17. Women in the sample ranged in age from 14 to 47; the mean age was 27 years and six months, with precisely half (50 per cent) aged between 20 and 29 years.

A clear majority of the women (79 per cent, n=263) were at six weeks or earlier gestation when they ordered pills from Women Help Women. Four out of five in the sample gave at least one reason why they needed an abortion; the majority (55 per cent) gave more than one reason. Reasons for needing an abortion were similar to those given in studies of women across a range of countries (Kirkman et al, 2009; Chae et al, 2017). Financial problems (38 per cent) were most often cited, followed by 'too soon' (27 per cent) and 'I feel I'm too young' (26 per cent), while 15 per cent said their family was complete, seven per cent cited health reasons and two per cent said the pregnancy was the result of rape. 'Other' reasons included: currently homeless/living with friends; Hyperemesis Gravida; and a range of issues in previous pregnancies including high blood pressure and pelvic girdle pain.

For the interviewees from Northern Ireland, the most common and concerning theme was fear. Given the legal regime outlined earlier, they feared that the pills would be seized by customs and they would not be able to end the pregnancy; they feared that they might need to seek medical assistance; some had believed they needed medical assistance, but had not sought it; and they cited a general fear of arrest and prosecution if anyone discovered what they were doing. As in Aiken et al's study (2017), positive themes also emerged from the interviews: relief at not having to travel to end the pregnancy, with the implications that may have for work and for childcare; and relief at no longer being pregnant.

Significantly, those who had used the pills prior to the launch of the prosecutions did not exhibit the same fear of prosecution or police involvement, although they avoided seeking medical assistance due to awareness that their actions were unlawful. Those who used pills after the prosecutions started in 2015 expressed much greater levels of fear. Given Martha's experience when the police arrived at her door, this fear is understandable.

> 'The bad thing [about the pills] was that mine never arrived. And that they were seized in customs. And it was just a nightmare thereafter that. Again I am not going to get into it, but with police and everything else, it was just horrendous.' (Martha, 38)

Most of the Northern Irish women were acutely conscious that what they were doing was illegal, which affected who they were willing to tell in case that person informed the police. Such concerns were exacerbated by the case noted earlier of the 21-year old woman given a three-month suspended prison sentence when her flatmates called the police after she disclosed that she had taken abortion pills:

> 'What if somebody then turns around and tells the police on you or something? And you are in the middle of this process and all of a sudden the police arrive at the door or something? That's a bit horrible as well. It makes you

kind of look at all your connections and your friendships in a bit of a different light. Which I think is so wrong. Like would we be doing that for any other medical procedure? No.' (Tracy, late 30s, five children)

A minority of women did not know that what they were doing was illegal; more precisely, they believed it was not lawful but, until the prosecutions started, did not appreciate that it was a crime:

'I suppose it was a bit ignorant of me … I didn't read that much into knowing that it was actually illegal. I knew that abortion wasn't offered here, but because it is part of the UK, I didn't think it was actually illegal. I just thought it's not offered here … but … as I say, I was that desperate I didn't see no other way.' (Laura, 24, no children, NI)

However, most of the women were clear that prosecution was something they were willing to risk because of the advantages provided by being able to self-manage the abortion.

'I knew that it was illegal. I was worried. But for all the spiral now about the people being taken to court and whatever else, I never thought on that. And I don't think it would have stopped me.' (Joan, late 40s, five children)

Some younger women recounted being frightened by the level of pain and bleeding they experienced. Yet, while concerned that they might need medical assistance, they did not seek it. This is alarming, since the pills' strong safety record is based on women being able to access medical help, for example, blood transfusions, if required. One young woman recounted:

'I turned round to my partner and was like, we need to go to the hospital. Even though I knew I couldn't go because what I had done was completely illegal. And

I was saying to him, and it was really dramatic because I kept thinking, I am going to die. I think I am going to die, we need to go to hospital. But he was like we can't. … Like you do get prosecuted and everything like that. But yeah, I wouldn't have gone for medical help, no.' (Marie, 19 at time of abortion)

By contrast, no participant from Scotland expressed such fears. The health impact of the abortion simply did not occur to them. Even when pressed on this issue, it was clear that they saw no reason to worry about themselves.

Given that the Northern Irish participants expressed such fears in self-managing their abortions, they were asked whether they would have travelled for a legal abortion had free NHS abortions been available when they took abortion pills outside the law. Their responses suggest that criminalisation does not deter the practice; it simply makes self-managing abortion outside of formal healthcare systems less safe. While some participants indicated that they would have travelled if money had not been an issue, the majority said that they would have used the pills anyway. Being unable to afford to take time off work was the main explanation. Using pills allowed these women to plan their abortion around their work schedule, whereas travelling, especially for those outside of Belfast, would mean taking at least two days off work. Childcare, being able to access an earlier abortion, and preventing an abusive partner from knowing about the termination were other reasons for not availing themselves of the free NHS abortions in England:

'I only needed to take one day off work and kind of planned it around when my kids weren't going to be here.' (Tracy, late 30s, five children)

'I was able to carry out the abortion far earlier … And at the same time I was able to stay at home. I wasn't having to go … and feel like an outcast … that discomfort of feeling that you are being … as I say, outcast, swept away over the sea.' (Sally, 22, one child)

These research findings offer a compelling demonstration of how criminalisation has failed to deter those seeking abortions outside the law and, further, has become an unsustainable policy position in an era where the internet provides easy access to safe pills to end an early pregnancy. Given the negative impact of criminalisation on women, it is unsurprising that in recent years Northern Ireland's abortion law has attracted extensive criticism and generated a range of legal challenges which form the backdrop to the 2019 reforms.

Human rights challenges to the criminalisation of abortion

In 2013, the Northern Ireland Human Rights Commission (NIHRC), established in 1999 as part of the Good Friday Agreement, expressed concern that abortion law in the jurisdiction was not compliant with the European Convention on Human Rights (ECHR). A joint consultation with the Department of Health was vetoed by then Northern Ireland Health Minister, Jim Wells (DUP), prompting the Department of Justice to move forward alone with a consultation on whether the law should be reformed to permit abortion in limited circumstances, namely 'if there has been a diagnosis that the fetus is a result of rape or where the fetus was diagnosed with a fatal fetal abnormality (FFA)' (Department of Justice, 2015). Ultimately the Department recommended legislation to allow terminations in cases of fatal fetal abnormality, but not rape. The refusal to permit a joint consultation also led the NIHRC to institute judicial review proceedings. It contended that the failure to provide for termination of pregnancy in cases where the pregnant woman was carrying a fetus with a serious malformation or a fatal fetal abnormality, or where her pregnancy was a result of rape/incest, breached Articles 3 (protection against inhuman and degrading treatment),

8 (protection of private and family life) and 14 (protection from discrimination) of the ECHR.

In November 2015 the High Court in Belfast ruled that Northern Irish law breached human rights in denying abortion to a woman carrying a fetus with a fatal abnormality or who had become pregnant as a result of rape (*Re NIHRC* 2015). In a subsequent judgment, to clarify aspects of the November decision, Horner J issued a declaration of incompatibility under the Human Rights Act (*Re NIHRC* 2015). An appeal by the Attorney General was allowed, primarily on the grounds that abortion was a matter for the legislature at Stormont (*Re NIHRC* 2017). However, on the substantive issue concerning the UK government's human rights obligations, the judges variously accepted that the law breached women's human rights. Weatherup LJ concurred with the High Court that current restrictions on access to abortion breached Article 8, while Morgan LCJ and Gillen LJ stated that women pregnant as a result of rape or having had a diagnosis of fetal anomaly *should* be entitled to treatment in Northern Ireland under the existing legal framework. Leave was granted to the NIHRC to appeal to the UK Supreme Court, which handed down its judgment in June 2018, shortly after citizens in the Republic of Ireland voted to Repeal the 8th Amendment, thus paving the way to partial decriminalisation south of the border (deLondras, forthcoming).

In a split decision (4–3), a majority of the Supreme Court ruled that the NIHRC lacked standing to bring the case without an actual or perceived victim and, consequently, that the Supreme Court lacked jurisdiction to make a declaration of incompatibility on the basis of its substantive conclusions (*Re NIHRC* 2018; Rooney, 2019a). What is important, however, is that once again and by a majority, the Court ruled that the law in Northern Ireland violated Article 8 in respect of women diagnosed with a fatal fetal abnormality (on this issue the split was 5–2), and in respect of women whose pregnancy resulted from rape or incest (4–3 split). Two judges also held that the current law breached Article 3. All were agreed that there was no breach of Articles 8 or 3 in respect of serious fetal abnormality cases and that there was no need to address the Article 14 claim that the law discriminated against women from Northern Ireland.

While the Supreme Court's judgment was damning, it went nowhere near as far as the earlier CEDAW report, which had found 'grave' and 'systematic' violations in relation to cases of severe fetal impairment (including FFA), and rape or incest, and 'systematic' violations in the criminalisation of abortion and highly restrictive access to services. CEDAW noted that the law wrongly compelled women to a) carry pregnancies to full term; b) travel outside of Northern Ireland to undergo legal abortions; or c) self-administer abortion with pills (CEDAW, 2018). In summary then, by 2018 it was clear that authoritative human rights and political bodies, as well as the UK's highest court, had accepted that Northern Ireland's abortion law was not human rights compliant. The key questions about effecting the necessary legal reforms concerned whether decriminalisation was the appropriate response, and who had responsibility for changing the law.

Law reform and the framework for regulating abortion

As regards legal responsibility for law reform, it is clear that the criminal law relating to abortion in Northern Ireland falls within the legislative competence of the Northern Ireland Assembly (section 4(1) Northern Ireland Act 1998). In 2018, the Secretary of State for Northern Ireland, Karen Bradley, told the Women and Equalities Committee that she was focused on the restoration of the Northern Ireland Assembly and Executive and that that was the most appropriate way to deal with abortion (Women and Equalities Committee, 2019: paras 71–2). However, the Assembly has been suspended since March 2017, and ultimate responsibility for remedying any breach of human rights norms rests with the UK government, which cannot devolve responsibility for compliance with its international obligations under international law (Women and Equalities Committee, 2019, chapters 4 and 5). This prompted Stella Creasy (Lab) to table an amendment to the Northern Ireland (Executive Formation and Exercise of Functions) Act in July 2019. The Act extended the period for Northern Ireland Ministers to be appointed until 21 October 2019 and required the Secretary of State for Northern Ireland to report to the Westminster Parliament on progress towards forming an Executive. The amendment, which passed by 332–99 votes in the House of Commons and 182–37 in the Lords, became section 9 of the 2019 Act. When it came into effect at midnight on 21 October, sections 58 and 59 of the Offences Against the Person Act 1861 were repealed and a moratorium was introduced on 'criminal proceedings … in respect of an offence under those sections under the law of Northern Ireland (whenever committed)' (sections 9(2) and (3)).

Notwithstanding the overwhelming support for this measure at Westminster, concerns have been raised regarding the absence of regulation in Northern Ireland for provision of abortion services. However, as in the case of Great Britain (Chapter Four), such concerns tend to ignore the legal frameworks that currently regulate health services in Northern Ireland. Far from a regulatory vacuum in the jurisdiction, abortion will instead be governed by the legal regulation and medical guidelines applicable to other healthcare procedures.

The general regulatory framework within which healthcare services are provided is broadly similar to that which applies elsewhere in the UK (Chapter Four). Notably, in Northern Ireland providers of any regulated activity are subject to similar detailed obligations governing the provision of safe care. The Regulation and Quality Improvement Authority (RQIA) is the equivalent of the Care Quality Commission. It has statutory responsibility for monitoring and regulating the quality of health and care services under the Health and Personal Social Services (Quality, Improvement and Regulation)

(Northern Ireland) Order 2003. This Order brought into effect arrangements equivalent to those which were already in place in England, Wales and Scotland, including powers to review and inspect the quality of services provided by the Department of Health, Social Services and Public Safety (DHSSPS). The Order places a statutory duty of quality on the Health and Social Care (HSC) Board, HSC Trusts and some special agencies with regard to provision of services; it requires the DHSSPS to develop standards against which the quality of services can be measured and makes provision for evaluating clinical and social care governance arrangements within HSC bodies, designed to underpin the statutory duty of quality placed upon them. While abortion services have not hitherto been subject to the requirements of this general framework in Northern Ireland, they can readily be incorporated now that abortion has been decriminalised. In this regard the 2003 Order explicitly entrusted RQIA with powers to develop and disseminate standards and guidelines for both regulated and non-regulated care services, including many services that previously had been unregulated. What is important is that the RQIA's powers extend to services delivered by both HSC Trusts and the independent sector (Art 38), enabling licensing, inspection and enforcement mechanisms to be put in place for abortion providers in each sector.

Clearly, the general common law provisions applicable to health professionals and the professional guidance outlined in Chapter Four apply throughout the UK. As noted there, 'the legal framework for ensuring high quality abortion care is largely to be found in the general provisions of law' (p 62) rather than in an abortion-specific law. Thus, health professionals in the jurisdiction are required to comply with general common law requirements regarding the need for valid informed consent and respect for confidentiality when they offer any health service. As regards minors, the Family Law Reform Act 1969 extends to Northern Ireland and the *Gillick* ruling applies. Likewise, the Mental Capacity Act

Northern Ireland 2016 offers substantially the same protections as the Mental Capacity Act 2005 regarding the termination of pregnancy where an adult woman lacks competence to give consent. Other ancillary legislation discussed in Chapter Four that touches upon how abortion is regulated also extends to Northern Ireland, including the Human Tissue Act 2004 and the General Data Protection Regulation 2018. Finally, the relevant professional guidance issued by the General Medical Council and Nursing and Midwifery Council discussed in Chapter Four – including guidance on consent, confidentiality, safeguarding and prescribing – likewise binds health professionals in Northern Ireland. Consequently, only registered and licensed health practitioners with appropriate training will be able legally to perform surgical abortions; while serious and persistent failures to follow professional guidance would place a health professional's registration at risk (McGuinness and Montgomery, 2019).

Similarly, as is explained in more detail in Chapter Four, in the wake of decriminalisation of abortion, the actions of all citizens, including health professionals, will continue to be circumscribed by the general criminal law. The Human Medicines Regulations 2012 apply throughout the UK, setting quality standards, and limiting the power to prescribe and supply regulated medications to those appropriately qualified and licensed. Non-consensual terminations can be prosecuted under the provisions of the Offences Against the Person Act 1861 that govern the causing or infliction of harm and poisoning (sections 18, 20, 23, 24, 47). Abortion in Northern Ireland will also remain subject to section 25 of the Criminal Justice Act, meaning that it remains a serious criminal offence to end the life of a viable fetus. As discussed previously, in practice this means where the pregnancy has reached 24 weeks.

Unlike the rest of the UK, given that the Abortion Act did not extend to Northern Ireland, there is currently no statutory right to conscientiously object to participating in treatment to end a pregnancy. There is, however, explicit reference to conscientious objection in the DHSSSP guidance, which provided that in a non-emergency situation 'no-one with moral/religious objections should be compelled to participate in a termination of pregnancy or handle fetal remains resulting from a termination of pregnancy' (DHSSPS, 2016: para 4.3). Trusts were instructed to put measures in place to accommodate the personal views of staff. Interim guidance from the NI Office has indicated that the new regulations will likely provide for conscientious objection, noting that the clause in the Abortion Act has been limited to direct involvement in the provision of abortion (NIO, 2019: 5–6). Of course, the relevant guidance from professional bodies, for example, the General Medical Council and Nursing and Midwifery Council also provide a level of protection to patients and health professionals.

The October 2019 reforms and the interim period

Shortly before abortion was decriminalised, on 3 October 2019, the Belfast High Court delivered its ruling on a judicial review brought by Sarah Ewart, one of the interveners in the Supreme Court case, who was subsequently granted permission to launch a judicial review in her own name (*Re Ewart* 2019). In 2013 Ms Ewart had received a diagnosis, when she was 12 weeks pregnant, that her unborn child had anencephaly, a fatal fetal abnormality, and was expected to die at birth or shortly thereafter. Denied an abortion in Northern Ireland, she had been forced to travel to England to end her pregnancy. While the Court accepted that she had standing to bring the case and concurred with the Supreme Court that the applicable law was incompatible with Article 8, it refused to make a formal declaration of incompatibility at that stage (Rooney, 2019b), given that the 2019 Act was due to come into force, as it duly did at midnight on 21 October.

No criminal prosecutions can now be brought against women who access, or health professionals who offer, abortion services within the framework outlined earlier in the chapter. The Westminster government is obliged to expeditiously change abortion laws in Northern Ireland by no later than 31 March 2020 to conform with the CEDAW recommendations (section 9(6)(7)). During this interim period women who purchase abortion medication online can seek aftercare without fear of criminal repercussions and existing cases will be dropped (NIO, 2019). Until the new regulations are in place, no additional services will be provided, but the NIO has issued guidance for health professionals. Anyone needing an abortion will have travel, accommodation and any costs incurred covered by the Westminster government and any health professional approached by a woman seeking termination should refer her to the Central Booking Service in England (NIO, 2019: 5; for criticism of the focus on travel in the guidance, see McGuinness and Montgomery, 2019).

A consultation process will shortly begin on the framing of regulations to govern abortion provision. The consensus among healthcare professionals appears to be that the provision of safe local abortion will likely entail that early medical abortion (EMA) is provided by GPs and/or family planning clinics, as in the Republic of Ireland. A good network of Contraceptive and Sexual Health (CASH) services exists as a basis for such provision, while EMA could be delivered via existing telemedicine services to rural areas (Horgan et al, 2019). The NIO guidance provides that the funding of abortions in England will continue until there is confidence 'that service provision in Northern Ireland is available to meet women's needs' (NIO, 2019: 5). For those who have medical issues or need a surgical abortion it is proposed that a limited number of hospitals across the region act as providers of second trimester services, including an estimated 40–50 post 20-week terminations each year (Horgan et al, 2019).

Conclusion

It is unlikely that the actual numbers of women accessing terminations will change significantly as a result of this decriminalisation of abortion in Northern Ireland (see further Chapter Six). Rather, the difference will lie in the fact that they can access abortion care locally, at an earlier gestational stage and without the fear and stigma which accompanies accessing services deemed unlawful. As we have shown, neither is decriminalisation liable to result in a regulatory free for all. In Northern Ireland, as in the rest of the UK, the general framework of statute and common law, supplemented by professional guidance, already offers a structure within which abortion services can be safely provided and effectively regulated, while a 24-week time limit remains in place. The key challenge in the interim period until March 2020 will lie, not in regulating the procedure, but in ensuring that an adequate range of services can be provided, notably as regards recruiting staff and funding provision.

SIX

What would be the likely impact of decriminalisation on the incidence, timing, provision and safety of abortion?

Brooke Ronald Johnson Jr, Louise Keogh and Wendy V. Norman

Introduction

What happens when criminal regulations and penalties for abortion are removed? Are there changes in incidence of abortion, in average gestational age at the time of abortion, in the nature or number of sex-selective abortions, in abortion safety or abortion access? Are there effective ways to ensure access and regulate safety?

Abortion is a common health procedure. Globally, roughly one in four pregnancies end in abortion (Sedgh et al, 2016). When done in a hygienic setting following evidence-based guidance for methods and care, abortion is also one of the safest health procedures for women (Ganatra et al, 2017). Abortion is as old as humanity and probably occurs in all cultures (David, 1981). However, despite its ubiquity and its safety, in most countries abortion continues to be regulated in criminal law. Some jurisdictions prohibit all abortions; some prohibit or penalise *unlawful* abortions and provide no information about lawful abortion; some allow or permit abortion on one or more specified grounds; some have decriminalised abortion to the extent of permitting it with no requirement for justification, but criminal sanctions may still apply if a gestational limit has been exceeded (Johnson et al, 2018). In a small number of jurisdictions, abortion has been fully decriminalised and is regulated as any other health intervention in the national or sub-national health system.

In this chapter we address issues that are seen by some as cause for concern in discussion on decriminalisation, including abortion incidence, timing, use for sex selection and safety. We present a brief overview of evidence from global data and then focus on two jurisdictions that have fully decriminalised abortion – the country of Canada and the State of Victoria, Australia. Each case study examines the process of decriminalisation and the subsequent effects on abortion incidence, timing, provision in the context of sex selection and safety. For each case study we present the socio-political context and nature of decriminalisation, significant changes in service access and availability following decriminalisation, and how these changes were addressed both politically, through subsequent legislation and court actions, and clinically through public health regulations.

Abortion laws, incidence, timing, provision and safety in global perspective

Abortion laws and criminalisation

Throughout the world, most countries use criminal laws to regulate the grounds, timing and provision of abortion. The cumulative effect of such regulations determines who has access to safe abortion and when, where, how and by whom services can be offered.

At the beginning of the twentieth century, abortion was legally restricted at all stages of pregnancy throughout most of Europe and North America (David, 1992). It was first legalised in the Russian Soviet Republic in 1920 (David, 1974). Iceland, Denmark and Sweden began liberalising their abortion laws in the 1930s. The 1950s, 1960s and 1970s saw a wave of laws expanding access to abortion, primarily in Soviet countries, Europe and North America (United Nations Department of Economic and Social Affairs, 2001–02). Today, approximately 50 countries permit abortion with no requirement for justification up to 12 or more weeks of fetal gestation (Lavelanet et al, 2018). Although abortion remains in the criminal code in nearly all of these countries, it is not a crime if performed according to national guidelines and within legally prescribed gestational limits.

Incidence of abortion

In 2010–2014, there were approximately 35 abortions per 1,000 women aged 15–44 years globally; 27 abortions per 1,000 in developed countries and 36 per 1,000 in developing countries, the difference due mainly to poorer access to and knowledge and availability of contraception and related reproductive health services in developing countries (Sedgh et al, 2016). Incidence of abortion is primarily a consequence of unintended pregnancy, usually resulting from ineffective or non-use of contraception (Singh et al, 2018).

No association has been found between the incidence of abortion and the grounds under which it is legal (Sedgh et al, 2016). Rather, the evidence suggests that the incidence of abortion depends on multiple factors including the availability and use of effective contraception, cultural norms related to desired family size and a host of social and economic factors (Sedgh et al, 2016). Differences in the accuracy of data reporting may affect the reliability of the reported incidence of abortion.

Apparent increases in abortion incidence following legal reform have occurred but have tended not to be sustained. The initial increase may reflect more reliable reporting as the proportion of lawful abortions increases and may be followed by a real decrease in incidence as contraceptive prevalence increases. In Romania, for example, when the law was changed in 1990 after more than 20 years of severe enforcement of a highly restrictive abortion law, the incidence of legal, safe abortion initially rose dramatically. However, the abortion rate dropped back to being in line with international norms following sustained improvements in sexual and reproductive health programmes and services, including access to and availability of effective contraception (Horga et al, 2013). Rates of illegal and unsafe abortion and maternal mortality declined rapidly and substantially (Stephenson et al, 1992; Johnson et al, 1993).

Gestational age at time of abortion

In most high-income countries with lawful abortion and reliable data, 90 per cent or more of abortions are performed at less than 13 weeks and two thirds at less than nine weeks gestational age (Popinchalk and Sedgh, 2019). The trend towards earlier abortion has paralleled a dramatic increase in the proportion performed with the drugs mifepristone and misoprostol (Popinchalk and Sedgh, 2019), which, subject to local laws and regulations, can be provided on an outpatient basis through primary care (WHO, 2012a; 2015). Increasing use of medical abortion is probably a result of a combination of factors, including individual choice, service provider preference, increased availability and affordability of mifepristone and misoprostol, and the desire – by both pregnant persons and governments – for abortions to be available through primary care.

Sex-selection and abortion

Contrary to the fears of some, the evidence is that decriminalisation is not statistically associated with sex-selective abortion. Prenatal sex diagnosis and sex-selective abortion have resulted in imbalanced sex ratios at birth in only ten countries – Albania, Armenia, Azerbaijan, China (including Hong Kong and Taiwan), Georgia, India, Republic of Korea, Montenegro, Tunisia and Vietnam (Chao et al, 2019) – despite most having laws in place that prohibit or severely restrict prenatal sex selection and/or sex-selective abortion (WHO, 2018).

Cultures in which female sex-selective abortion is most prominent tend to be those with marked gender inequities, independent of criminal law. Use of female sex-selective abortion may be exacerbated by the aforementioned sociocultural phenomena as well as population policies, such as China's former one-child policy, and declining fertility, which limits the scope for people's ideals related to small family size and sex composition (WHO, 2011; Chao et al, 2019). Criminalising or otherwise restricting abortion for sex selection or any other reason simply drives individuals to seek unsafe abortion providers and practices (WHO, 2012a).

Safety of abortion

Safe abortion requires accurate information, knowledgeable and skilled provision, and use of WHO-recommended methods, including vacuum aspiration, combination mifepristone and misoprostol, or dilatation and evacuation, depending on an individual's choice, method availability and fetal gestational age (Ganatra et al, 2017). Two analyses of abortion data from the United States between 1988–2005 showed that mortality from safe, legal abortion was only 0.7 and 0.6 per 100,000 abortion procedures, respectively (Bartlett et al, 2004; Raymond and Grimes, 2012), making abortion in the US safer than receiving an injection of penicillin (Cates, 2003; WHO, 2012a).

The proportion of safe abortions is significantly higher in developed countries and in countries with less restrictive abortion laws. Between 2010 and 2014 an estimated 45 per cent of all abortions remained unsafe, with 97 per cent of these occurring in developing countries (Ganatra et al, 2017).

Decriminalising abortion

According to the WHO: '[r]estricting legal access to abortion does not decrease the need for abortion, but it is likely to increase the number of women seeking illegal and unsafe abortions, leading to increased morbidity and mortality' (WHO, 2012a). Furthermore, '[l]aws, policies and practices that restrict access to abortion information and services can deter women from care seeking and create a "chilling effect" (suppression of actions because of fear of reprisals or penalties) for the provision of safe, legal services' (WHO, 2012a). Legal restrictions also result in inequalities of access since the more affluent can often obtain safe services by paying private providers or travelling to a jurisdiction where the abortion service is lawful (WHO, 2012a).

Although a large number of countries have partially decriminalised abortion, laws expanding access are often written vaguely, creating uncertainty, and may even conflict with what is allowed in practice (Erdman and Johnson, 2018). The following case studies are of two jurisdictions that have fully decriminalised abortion. Their contexts have a number of similarities. Like the UK, both rank highly on a broad range of socioeconomic and health indicators. They also reflect comparatively high levels of contraceptive prevalence and low incidence of abortion. Canada repealed criminal provisions related to abortion in 1988 and Victoria in 2008.

Case study 1: Abortion in Canada

Canada is the only country in the world to have fully decriminalised abortion. The former criminal law relating to abortion was struck down by the Supreme Court of Canada on 28 January 1988. Abortion has since been governed through health regulations. Following decriminalisation, the abortion rate has not risen and remains lower than the current rate in England and Wales.

To understand the consequences of decriminalisation, we explore the context relating to abortion regulation in Canada from the time abortion first became lawful in 1969, through to complete decriminalisation in 1988, and forward 30 years to 2018. We examine changes leading to and from the act of decriminalisation, in particular health regulations that govern abortion in the absence of a criminal law and particular aspects of abortion service delivery following decriminalisation. We also address questions about the epidemiology of abortion in Canada: did decriminalisation affect the incidence of abortion, gestational age at the time of abortion, the incidence of sex-selective abortion, and abortion safety? Further, we discuss unique service access issues in Canada related to geography and the lack of a single unified health system.

Historical context

In 1969 the Federal government changed the Criminal Code to permit abortion if certain conditions were met. Abortions were required to be performed in a hospital, approved by the facility's Therapeutic Abortion Committee (Government of Canada, 1969), and reported to the federal statistics agency.

The opportunity to decriminalise abortion in Canada arose in 1982 when the Federal government implemented a new constitutional amendment, *The Charter of Rights and Freedoms* (Government of Canada, 1982). In 1988 the Supreme Court of Canada ruled that the abortion provision in the criminal code violated a person's right to life, liberty and security of person under section 7 of this new Charter (*R v Morgentaler* 1988). With the loss of the federal law, by default abortion services became regulated in the same way as other medical care (Norman and Downie, 2017; Shaw and Norman, 2019). The Canadian Medical Association (CMA) provided guidelines which supported abortion provision by physicians in either hospital or non-hospital facilities and stressed the importance of early referral, collegial relations between professionals, and unimpeded access (CMA, 1988).

Abortion regulation post-decriminalisation

Since 1988 Canadian governments and health decision makers have attempted to use three main approaches to ensure the regulation of abortion service provision:

- federal criminal law;
- provincial health system legislation; and
- health system regulation by the licensing bodies for health professionals and by hospital accreditation systems.

Healthcare funding in Canada flows from the Federal government to the provinces along with direction on which healthcare services must be provided for all residents, as stipulated in the Canada Health Act 1985 (Martin et al, 2018). However, the organisation and delivery of healthcare services is managed by each of the provinces independently and also by a range of federal health systems serving specific populations (for example, military, refugees, aboriginal peoples). Similarly, the regulation of the scope of practice of healthcare professionals is provided by independent provincial licensing bodies, and the accreditation of the services performed by healthcare professionals is managed either by hospital-based privileging systems within each hospital, or by the provincial licensing bodies for community-based facilities.

Provincial legislation on abortion post-decriminalisation

Notwithstanding many attempts to recriminalise abortion, no replacement federal law has been passed (Abortion Rights Coalition of Canada, 2018), thus abortion provision became a provincial matter. Some provinces initially introduced some legislation to restrict provision of abortion, however courts across Canada found these measures to be unconstitutional (Erdman et al, 2017). Within a decade after the 1988 Supreme Court decision most of the 13 provinces and territories introduced legislation to guarantee access to abortion (DGPSCF, 1995; Access to Abortion Services Act 1995 (British Columbia); Desmarais, 1999).

Health system regulation governs abortion services post-decriminalisation

Abortion care remains regulated in Canada, in a manner consistent with the regulation of other health services, irrespective of decriminalisation. Canadian provincial health systems regulate health professionals through provincial government appointed licensing bodies (College of Physicians and Surgeons of Ontario, 2019). These bodies stipulate the medical acts that are within the scope of each profession and require registrants to practice within the limits of their training, experience and personal competence. Until 2017, abortion provision had been solely within the defined scope of practice for physicians. Shortly after the 2017 introduction of mifepristone, the medical abortion pill, the regulators of nursing practice across Canada determined medical abortion provision to be within the scope of nurse practitioner registrants (College of Nurses of Ontario, 2017).

Regulation of surgical services provided in hospitals or community-based surgical facilities

Hospitals are responsible for the establishment of guidelines regarding the accreditation of their healthcare staff, programmes, specific services and medical procedures. Since the risk of complications of abortion increases with gestational age (Ferris et al, 1996; Dunn et al, 2011; Grimes and Creinin, 2004), such accreditation typically establishes an upper gestational age for provision of abortion, either by a healthcare professional or for a facility as a whole, and often for both. Similar accreditation standards are established individually for non-hospital-based procedure facilities through the provincial health professional licensing bodies (College of Physicians and Surgeons of British Columbia, 2019).

Gestational age limits at facilities in Canada

A 2012 national survey of abortion facilities found that 44 per cent offered surgical abortion for a gestational age limit at 14 weeks or higher; a few offered services up to 24 weeks; about a quarter mandated a limit of 12 weeks; and fewer than one in ten limited gestational age at or under 11 weeks (Norman et al, 2016). At that time in Canada the median gestational age among hospital-performed abortions was less than 10 weeks (CIHI, 2014). Abortion care beyond 24 weeks is possible on a case-by-case basis at some Canadian facilities or through referral to facilities in the United States.

Abortion incidence, timing, provision, and safety post-decriminalisation

In this section, we examine the evidence before and after decriminalisation for:

- incidence of abortion
- maternal age and gestational age at the time of abortion
- incidence of sex-selective abortion
- safety of abortion

Incidence of abortion

Surveillance of the incidence of abortion in Canada was impeded and resulted in significant underreporting until about 1992. During the period from 1969 to decriminalisation in

1988 the government reported all hospital-based abortions, but community-based abortion – being illegal though widely practised – evaded surveillance. Hospital abortions for some patients in the privileged classes also bypassed regulatory restrictions where they were reported as miscarriage management (Wilcox et al, 1981; Johnson et al, 2005). Abortions in both of these categories rapidly began to be captured in data in the years immediately following decriminalisation, from 1989 to 1992. Thus, although the incomplete capture of abortions prior to decriminalisation indicated a rate of 10–12 per 1,000 females aged 15–44, the rate captured by 1992 of 15 per 1,000 females aged 15–44 is likely to represent the true incidence prior to decriminalisation (Norman, 2012). From 1992 the rate of abortion has been stable or declining in Canada and in 2016, the latest year available at time of press and thought to be a year of excellent data capture, it remained at just under 14 per 1,000 females aged 15–44 (Abortion Rights Coalition of Canada, 2013; CIHI, 2019; Statistics Canada, 2019). Abortion rates in Canada since decriminalisation for all years up to 2016 were lower than the abortion rate of 16 per 1,000 females aged 15–44 in England and Wales in 2016 (DHSC, 2018a).

Gestational and maternal age at abortion

Comprehensive data on gestational age at the time of abortion in Canada is available exclusively from hospital administrative databases and is reported through CIHI (2012; 2019). Community-based abortion clinics and medical abortions provided in primary-care facilities tend to be at lower gestational ages than those performed in hospitals (where for example, nearly all abortions over 16 weeks gestational age are performed). Thus, the hospital-only statistics reported by CIHI report a higher than true median gestational age at the time of abortion. CIHI data from 2016 report a median gestational age of nine weeks (CIHI, 2019), which is thus the upper end of the estimated range for median gestational age.

In Canada more than 90 per cent of reported abortions occur in the first trimester of pregnancy (CIHI, 2019). Individuals aged 18 to 29 account for nearly half of all procedures. Among those obtaining an abortion, approximately half have previously given birth (Dunn et al, 2011; CIHI, 2019) and the same proportion report having used contraception during the cycle when they became pregnant (Norman et al, 2011; Ames and Norman, 2012; Norman et al, 2014). Only hospitals provide abortion over 20 weeks gestational age, which in the majority of cases are related to fetal abnormalities. Across Canada only 0.6 per cent of all abortions occur beyond 20 weeks gestational age, and this proportion has been stable since decriminalisation (CIHI, 2012; 2014; 2019).

Incidence of sex-selective abortion

As seen in Figure 6.1, the sex ratio of males to females born in Canada to mothers born in Canada has been normal and did

Figure 6.1: Proportion of births that are male in Canada: trends over time for mothers born in Canada vs mothers born in India, 1990–2011

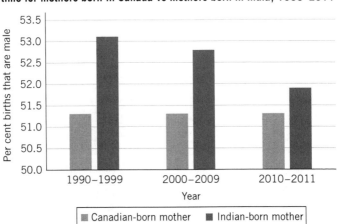

Source: Adapted from data tables in Urquia et al, 2016.

not change with decriminalisation of abortion in 1988 (Urquia et al, 2016). Higher rates of sex-selective abortion are seen among Indian-born mothers in Canada (see Figure 6.1). These effects are not significant for first- or second-born children, but one study suggests they may favour males among the much rarer (fewer than 14 per cent of births in Canada) third- or fourth-born children of mothers born in India (Urquia et al, 2016). The rate of 'missing girls' in this group has been declining in Canada since 2000.

Safety of abortion

The safety of abortion in Canada is well documented. Linked health administrative data analyses of the comprehensive single payer health system indicate that abortion services since decriminalisation have been delivered with a high degree of safety. During the period from decriminalisation to 2016, prior to the introduction of the medical abortion pill, nearly all abortions were provided as surgical procedures and very few required any subsequent care or hospitalisation. For procedures shortly after decriminalisation (1992–93), Ferris and colleagues examined all abortions in Canada's largest province and found an overall complication rate of 0.7 per cent (Ferris et al, 1996). Similarly, about a decade later as part of the provincial women's health project 'POWER', Dunn and colleagues confirmed that only 0.4 per cent of patients required admission to hospital within two weeks of an abortion and fewer than 5 per cent required any healthcare visit in the first two weeks post-abortion (Dunn et al, 2011). Examining data over the decade leading up to 2015, Liu and colleagues found that 0.1 per cent of patients having an abortion had serious complications, with about 1 per cent reporting any complication (Liu et al, 2019). These rates of serious complications for abortion compare favourably to those related to birth, with about an eight-fold higher mortality risk at the time of delivery compared to those reported by Liu et al for abortion (Joseph et al, 2010).

Canadian-specific challenges to provide access to abortion

One factor to consider when examining the potential effect of decriminalisation is whether it would improve access to safe abortion care. Canada's main challenges to access are not related to federal decriminalisation but rather reflect two other factors: the extensive geographic disparity between where people live and where healthcare is delivered; and two isolated persistent cases of provincial legislation that sought to limit access to abortion.

For the first, Canada's geographic disparity is illustrated in Figure 6.2. Prior to official introduction of mifepristone in 2017, over 96 per cent of abortions were provided surgically (Norman et al, 2016). Nearly 90 per cent of all abortions were provided in the largest cities (the census metropolitan areas, roughly the darkest shaded areas in Figure 6.2) and most of these were within 150 km of Canada's southern border (Kaposy, 2010). Yet it is estimated that fewer than 60 per cent of reproductive age females live in these dense urban areas and their distribution is similar to the areas with hospital services (the dots in Figure 6.2). As the inset map demonstrates, Canada's expansive geography and population distribution sets the challenges of service distribution apart from more densely populated countries such as the UK.

Summary

Abortion was decriminalised in Canada over 30 years ago. Following decriminalisation, the abortion rate did not rise substantially and remains lower than current rates in England and Wales; nor did gestational age at the time of abortion increase. Abortions performed beyond 20 weeks remain exceedingly rare, are predominantly due to fetal anomalies, and the rate has not risen since decriminalisation. Sex ratios at birth remain normal in Canada since decriminalisation. Abortion safety has steadily improved since decriminalisation. Following the removal of specific criminal prohibitions against abortion, abortion has been successfully governed by health

Figure 6.2: Canada's health services distribution challenge

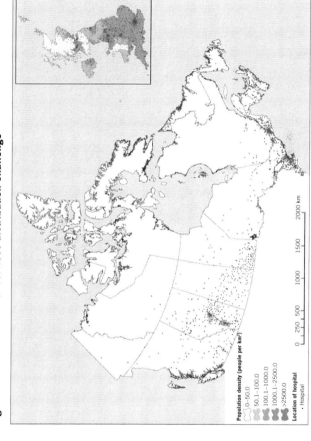

Source: Martin et al, 2018, reprinted with permission from Elsevier.

regulations. Several unsuccessful attempts have been made to propose new criminal sanctions, with one government bill and dozens of private member's bills. Initially provincial legislatures attempted to provide restrictive regulations; however, all have been revoked and largely replaced with supportive regulations. These supportive regulatory and health system policies have improved an equitable, accessible, abortion service. Canada has clearly demonstrated over three decades that abortion care can be safely and ethically regulated within the usual health system approach for other general reproductive health services, in the absence of a criminal law.

Case study 2: Abortion in Victoria, Australia

This case study describes the legal changes that were made to decriminalise abortion in the state of Victoria, Australia in 2008, the subsequent changes to legislation and regulation, and the impact of this change on abortion services and how women use them. Victoria does not routinely release state-wide data related to abortion due to limitations in the way procedures are recorded, but available data and published research are analysed to provide an indication of trends and patterns pre- and post-decriminalisation.

State-level regulation of abortion in Australia

Abortion law in Australia is managed at the state or territory level, as there is no federal law regulating abortion. However, surgical abortion is funded federally in the form of a Medicare rebate, and medical abortion has been listed on the Pharmaceutical Benefits Scheme since 2013, which means that it is partially subsidised by the Federal government. In states where abortion remains in the Crimes Act, it is provided subject to the Menhennit ruling (*R v Davidson* 1969). This means that in practice, abortion is available if deemed necessary to save the life of the woman.

As of September 2019, six of the eight states and territories had decriminalised abortion, creating a new piece of legislation for abortion in each state, including a clause regulating conscientious objection (Table 6.1). In a further state (South Australia), the South Australian Law Reform Institute is considering how the laws in that state should be updated to reflect current practice. Those states that decriminalised abortion more recently, Tasmania (TAS) in 2013, the Northern Territory (NT) in 2017, and Queensland (QLD) in 2018 included as part of the decriminalisation bill, safe access zones (or buffer zones) to prevent protests within 150 metres of services. In states where abortion was decriminalised earlier, Australian Capital Territory (ACT) in 2002 and Victoria (VIC) in 2008, bills to enforce safe access zones were introduced

Table 6.1: Authors' own summary of progress on decriminalisation in each state and territory in Australia

State/territory	Population ('000,000) 2017	Decriminalisation (date of first bill)	Safe access zones bills	Routine reporting of data	Abortion must occur in specified facility
New South Wales	7.9	2019	2018	✓	✓ (post 22-weeks)
Victoria	6.3	2008	2015	✗	✗
Queensland	4.9	2018	Included 2018	✗	✗
South Australia	1.7	✗	✗	✓	✓
West Australia	2.6	✗	✗	✗	✓
Tasmania	0.52	2013	Included 2013	✗	✗
Northern Territory	0.25	2017	Included 2017	✗	✗
Australian Capital Territory	0.41	2002	2015, 2018	✗	✓

subsequently. South Australia (SA) liberalised abortion in 1969, and while it is yet to fully decriminalise, it is the only state in Australia that routinely reports data related to abortion.

As well as a range of differences in the laws, there are also differences in how the laws are implemented. For example, gestational age limits vary, SA has a residency requirement, and in SA, ACT and Western Australia (WA) abortion can only be performed in certain facilities, while this limitation does not apply in other states. These legal, policy and regulatory variations between jurisdictions are thought 'to create uncertainty for women and providers' (de Moel-Mandel and Shelley, 2017: 121), and some have called for the creation of consistent laws across the country (de Costa and Douglas, 2015).

Decriminalisation of abortion in Victoria

In 2008, laws regulating abortion in Victoria were reformed (Abortion Law Reform Act 2008), rendering abortion provided by registered health practitioners (defined in the Act) a matter for health regulation, removing abortion from the criminal code and allowing abortion with no requirement for justification up to 24 weeks of gestation. After 24 weeks, abortion can be performed only if the medical practitioner reasonably believes that it is appropriate with regard to all relevant medical circumstances and the woman's current and future physical, psychological and social circumstances, and provided that he or she has consulted at least one other medical practitioner who also deems it to be appropriate in all of these circumstances. The law includes a provision (Section 8) on conscientious objection, mandating that doctors with a conscientious objection must refer patients to a service provider without a conscientious objection. The stated intent of these reforms was to shift decision making about abortion from doctors operating as gatekeepers to women being treated as competent decision makers. In 2015, further legislation was passed to establish 150 metre zones around health services in which protests cannot occur (Public Health and Wellbeing Amendment (Safe Access Zones) Act, 2015: s. 5), in an attempt to reduce the negative impact of protesters on both service providers' and women's experience.

Abortion services are provided through a mix of public and private hospitals and day-procedure centres. Not all public hospitals provide abortion services, as some of the major public teaching hospitals in Victoria are run by Catholic organisations that claim an institutional conscientious objection to the provision of abortion, as do some private hospitals. The provision of abortion services in any geographic region of Victoria is dependent on willing institutions and providers and is not governed by policy at the state or federal level. In 2018, the state government supported the development of 1800 My Options, a state-wide service providing information about contraception, pregnancy options and sexual health. Figure 6.3 provides a visual depiction of the location of publicly listed services in Victoria as captured by 1800 My Options and suggests that despite 30 per cent of the population residing outside of metropolitan Melbourne, there are large parts of the state without surgical services. While the number of medical abortion providers is increasing, they do not yet cover all parts of the state. Medical abortion services are likely to be under-represented in Figure 6.3, as some practices offer medical abortion, but choose to be registered privately with 1800 My Options. In addition, Marie Stopes provides medical abortion by telephone to women who live within two hours of 24-hour emergency medical care (www.mariestopes.org.au/abortion/home-abortion/). Only two services (a hospital and clinic in metropolitan Melbourne) provide abortions at 20 weeks of gestation or later.

A qualitative study conducted with abortion experts including service providers, counsellors, nurses and service managers in Victoria to explore the impact of decriminalisation on access to abortion found that, overall, law reform had been positive

Figure 6.3: Victorian abortion services listed on the 1800 My Options website

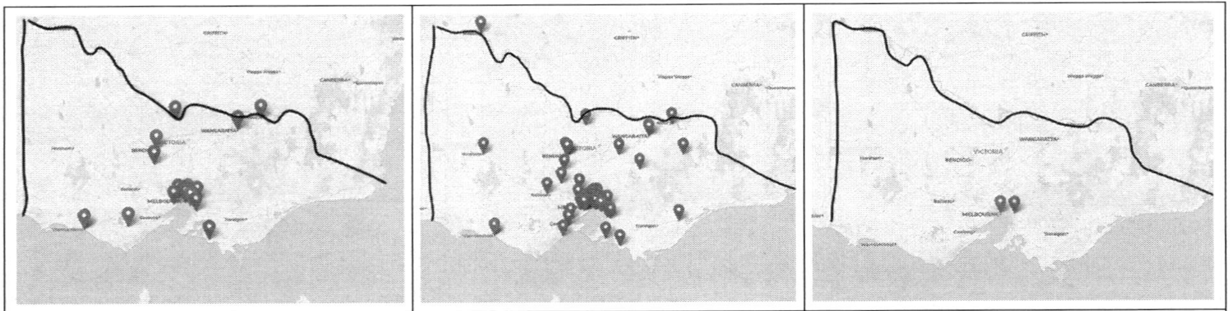

| Surgical abortion services (n=17) | Medical abortion services (n=30+) | Post 20 week abortion services (n=2) |

Source: Images reprinted with permission from www.1800myoptions.org.au/information/where-to-go (26 June 2019).

but much 'unfinished business' remained (Keogh et al, 2017). Concerns were raised around continued inequitable access to abortion services, especially a sense that both public services and abortions at later gestations had decreased in availability since law reform, primarily due to institutional opting out and ongoing stigma. Experts agreed that decriminalisation of abortion was 'a necessary but not sufficient step towards ensuring that women have equitable access to safe and appropriate abortion services' (Keogh et al, 2017).

Availability of abortion data

There is no nationally coordinated data collection or analysis in Australia, so attempts to study trends in abortion use are limited to South Australian data, *ad hoc* releases of data from state-level authorities, and published research evidence. Victoria collects data and reports on any death of a fetus over 20 weeks gestational age, including due to abortion, and these data can be analysed to determine pre- and post-decriminalisation trends in post-20-week abortions. Routine reporting from South Australia shows that since 1999 there has been a steady decline in the rate of pregnancy terminations, from 17.9 per 1,000 women aged 15–44 in 1999 to 13.2 in 2016. Furthermore, in SA, only 2.8 per cent of terminations are performed at 20 weeks of gestation or later. Of the 120 pregnancy terminations performed at 20 weeks of gestation or later in 2016, 58 (48 per cent) were for the mental health of the woman, 52 (43 per cent) were for congenital anomalies, and 10 (8 per cent) for specified medical conditions (Pregnancy Outcome Unit, 2018).

Abortion incidence, timing, provision and safety post-decriminalisation

Incidence of abortion

Similar to South Australia, it appears that the overall abortion rate in Victoria is on a steady downward trend, unaffected by

Table 6.2: Abortion rate per 1,000 Victorian women aged 15–44 years (including data for planned and unplanned abortions, for all reasons, from public and private hospitals and day procedure centres)

	2008	2017
Abortion rate per 1,000 women, 15–44	16.8	12.2

Source: Termination of Pregnancy Bill 2018. Report No. 11, 56th Parliament, Health, Communities, Disability Services and Domestic and Family Violence Prevention Committee, October 2018.

the decriminalisation of abortion in 2008. In 2018, selected data were released by the Victoria Minister of Health to the Queensland Law Reform Commission to support their review of termination of pregnancy laws (Table 6.2). The minister noted, however, that the rate reported includes procedures performed for medical reasons such as miscarriage or fetal death in-utero.

Medical termination of pregnancy (MTOP) was not widely available in Australia until 2013 when it was approved by the Pharmaceutical Benefits Scheme. It is possible to compare the number of MTOP prescriptions in Victoria, where abortion has been decriminalised with those in New South Wales, where it has not, as presented in Figure 6.4. There is no evidence that the number of prescriptions has been higher in Victoria due to the decriminalisation of abortion.

Gestational age at abortion

Abortions that are performed after 20 weeks of gestation in Victoria can be tracked over time through data reported by the Victorian Consultative Council on Obstetric and Paediatric Mortality and Morbidity (CCOPMM, 2011, 2012, 2014, 2017a, 2017b). Data have been extracted from reports and are presented in Figure 6.5. Abortions performed after 20 weeks for what are referred to in reports as 'maternal psychosocial' reasons increased steadily from 2000 to 2004, well prior to

Figure 6.4: Number of prescriptions for mifepristone and misoprostol in Victoria and New South Wales

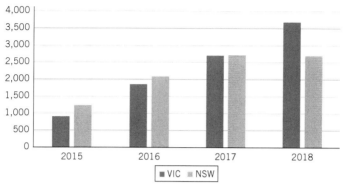

Source: Pharmaceutical Benefits Scheme reports on number of prescriptions by state and calendar year (data on item 10211K, http://medicarestatistics.humanservices.gov.au/statistics/pbs_item.jsp, accessed 11 July 2019).

Figure 6.5: Trend in the number of abortions performed at 20 weeks or later by reason in Victoria

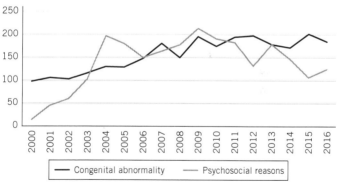

Source: Data extracted from reports from the Victorian Consultative Council on Obstetric and Paediatric Mortality and Morbidity (CCOPMM), 2011, 2012, 2014, 2017a, 2017b.

decriminalisation. Since 2009, abortions after 20 weeks of gestation for psychosocial reasons have been on a downward trend, while in contrast, abortions after 20 weeks due to a congenital abnormality have increased slightly. An influential factor in the number of abortions performed is the presence of healthcare providers willing or able to perform abortions after 20 weeks for psychosocial reasons. Since late abortions are controversial and require practised skills, willing and competent providers are few, and hospitals can elect only to perform abortions at later gestations for congenital abnormalities. Women requiring late abortion are often required to travel to another state or even to another country to access a safe service. Not all of the abortions reported in Figure 6.5 will have been for Victorian women and they are likely to also reflect the availability of private providers, so the numbers must be interpreted with caution. For example, if there are only two private providers offering post-20-week abortions for 'maternal psychosocial reasons' in Australia, and one is practising in Victoria, then the Victorian rate may seem inflated as women from other states travel to access the service. Abortions due to congenital abnormalities are likely to be rising due to the increased number of antenatal genetic tests offered to women during pregnancy.

Sex-selective abortion

Overall there has not been a significant increase in the male-to-female ratio in Victoria over the period 1999 to 2015 (Table 6.3). There are some data indicating that the male-to-female ratio has increased for children born to immigrant Indian and Chinese women with two or more children (Edvardsson et al, 2018) but it is not possible to determine the proportion of sex selection that is achieved through abortion compared to assisted reproduction. Edvardsson and colleagues (2018) postulate that the likely reasons for the increases in the male-to-female ratio over time among higher-parity

Table 6.3: Male-to-female ratio in Victorian births by time period, 1999–2015

Time period	n males/n females	Male/female ratio
1999–2004	193,053/183,606	1.051
2005–2010	219,047/207,651	1.055
2011–2015	198,978/188,291	1.057

Source: Data from personal communication with Kristina Edvardsson, as an extension of the data reported in Table 4 of Edvardsson et al, 2018: 2033.

Chinese- and Indian-born women include: the introduction of non-invasive prenatal testing (NIPT), which allows for accurate identification of fetal sex at an early gestation, and the significant drop in fertility following migration, which can increase the tendency to turn to prenatal sex selection to increase the chance of a male birth prior to completing the family. There is no evidence to support the suggestion that the decriminalisation of abortion has had any impact on the use of sex-selective abortion (if occurring) in these communities. Moreover, these slight male-to-female birth ratios fall within what may be considered a normally occurring level of imbalance (DHSC, 2019b).

Safety of abortion

A recent Victorian population-level observational study of all public and private hospital admissions (including day cases) had as a secondary aim to compare incident rates of surgical procedures and calculate their perioperative mortality rates (Fehlberg et al, 2019). Researchers reported surgical procedures published in the WHO Global Health Estimates categorisation of disease. The three most frequent procedures performed in Victoria during the three-year study period (2014–2016) were lens procedures (162,835), caesarean deliveries (76,032) and abortions with operating room procedure (65,451). The mortality rate for abortions with operating room procedure was 0 per cent compared to 0.0001 per cent for lens procedures and 0.01 per cent for caesarean deliveries, indicating that abortion was one of the safest surgical procedures conducted in Victoria from 2014 to 2016.

Summary

There is no evidence to indicate that the decriminalisation of abortion in Victoria had any impact on the abortion rate, the proportion of abortions performed at later gestations, or the use of sex-selective abortion. Indeed, decriminalisation appears to bear little relation to the provision of abortion services in Australia, which rather relies on appropriately trained and willing providers in supportive health systems. Decriminalisation did not explicitly address the sustainability of the workforce nor the number or geographic distribution of services.

Conclusion

Abortion results from both intended and unintended pregnancies that for one or multiple reasons become unwanted. Global data show clearly that abortions occur in all countries and regardless of legal regime. When abortions are restricted either in law or in practice, they are much more likely to be unsafe.

Increases in abortion incidence, gestational age and sex-selective abortion, often coupled with decreasing safety, are commonly cited by persons and groups opposed to abortion as unwelcome outcomes of legal reform. However, contrary to these assertions, evidence shows that levels of abortion incidence, gestational age, provision for sex selection and safety result from complex dynamics between pregnant persons and the social, cultural, political and economic context in which they live.

Findings from the case studies on Canada and Victoria, Australia are similar to what is seen globally. Based on existing reporting, peer-reviewed research findings and modelled estimates, the findings are that decriminalisation of abortion:

- does not directly increase the incidence of abortion;
- does not directly increase the gestational age at the time of abortion;
- does not directly affect the male-to-female ratio at birth; and,
- does not negatively affect the safety of abortion.

Indeed, decriminalisation has relatively little to do with these issues whose primary determinants include access to, availability, acceptability and quality of sexual and reproductive health information, education and services, and sociocultural norms that value and promote the health and rights of girls, women and all pregnant people.

Decriminalisation of abortion and moving its regulation to the health system can eliminate fears and stigma associated with potential criminal sanctions while enhancing individuals' autonomy, equality, dignity and privacy. However, providing equitable access to safe abortion – across diverse geographical, cultural, health, gender and socioeconomic strata – requires dedicated and sufficient public health resources and protective regulations to support prevention of unintended pregnancy, and to ensure that no pregnant person is ever forced to seek an unsafe abortion.

Notes

Chapter Three

[1] Mean age of women having an abortion is 27.4 years (DHSC, 2019a).

Chapter Four

[1] In the use and disposal of fetal tissue, all service providers would also be required to conform to the requirements of the Human Tissue Act (2004), or Human Tissue Act (Scotland) (2006) in the case of Scotland, and associated codes of practice.

References

Abortion Rights Coalition of Canada (2013) 'The Morgentaler decision: the struggle for abortion rights', Toronto, Canada: Abortion Rights Coalition of Canada. Available from: www.morgentaler25years.ca/the-struggle-for-abortion-rights/ [Accessed 31 May 2019].

Adamczyk, A. and Valdimarsdóttir, M. (2018) 'Understanding Americans' abortion attitudes: the role of the local religious context', *Social Science Research*, 71: 129–44.

Aiken, A.R.A., Gomperts, R. and Trussell, J. (2017) 'Experiences and characteristics of women seeking and completing at-home medical termination of pregnancy through online telemedicine in Ireland and Northern Ireland: a population-based analysis', *BJOG*, 124: 1208–15.

Aiken, A.R.A., Guthrie, K.A., Schellekens, M., et al (2018) 'Barriers to accessing abortion services and perspectives on using mifepristone and misoprostol at home in Great Britain', *Contraception*, 97: 177–83.

Ames, C.M. and Norman, W.V. (2012) 'Preventing repeat abortion in Canada: is the immediate insertion of intrauterine devices post abortion a cost-effective option associated with fewer repeat abortions?', *Contraception*, 85: 51–5.

Amnesty International (2014) *Attitudes to Abortion in NI*. Available from: www.amnesty.org.uk/files/milward_brown_poll_results_october_2014_final_0.pdf?sLBAl1wDBktydVn2rPlpLRz7Wqh0LvbZ [Accessed 31 October 2019].

Amnesty International (2015) *Barriers to Accessing Abortion Services.* Available from: www.amnesty.org/en/documents/eur45/1057/2015/en/ [Accessed 31 October 2019].

Amnesty International (2016) *Attitudes to Abortion in NI.* Available from: https://amnesty.org.uk/files/millward_brown_report_of_public_opinion_research_oct_2016.pdf?nP2thVJzOUNNwBthwikkJ_UM_PQmoAKO [Accessed 31 October 2019].

ANSIRH (Advancing New Standards in Reproductive Health) (2019) *Turnaway Study.* Available from: www.ansirh.org/research/turnaway-study [Accessed 31 October 2019].

AoMRC (Academy of Medical Royal Colleges) (2011) *Induced Abortion and Mental Health,* London: Academy of Medical Royal Colleges. Available from: www.aomrc.org.uk/wp-content/uploads/2016/05/Induced_Abortion_Mental_Health_1211.pdf [Accessed 31 October 2019].

APPG (All-Party Parliamentary Group on Population, Development and Reproductive Health) (2018) *Who Decides? We Trust Women: Abortion and the Developing World. A Report,* UK, March 2018. Available from: www.appg-popdevrh.org.uk/APPG%202018%20AW.pdf [Accessed 31 October 2019].

Autorino, T., Mattioli, F. and Mencarini, L. (2018) 'The impact of gynecologists' conscientious objection on access to abortion in Italy'. Available from: ftp://ftp.dondena.unibocconi.it/WorkingPapers/Dondena_WP119.pdf [Accessed 31 October 2019].

Ballantyne, A., Gavaghan, C. and Snelling, J. (2019) 'Doctors' rights to conscientiously object to refer patients to abortion service providers', *New Zealand Medical Journal,* 132: 64–71.

Bar Ngo, T.D., Park, M.H., Shakur, H. (2011) 'Comparative effectiveness, safety and acceptability of medical abortion at home and in a clinic: a systematic review', *Bulletin of the World Health Organization,* 89: 360–70. Available from: https://www.who.int/bulletin/volumes/89/5/10-084046/en/ [Accessed 12 December 2019].

Barkan, S.E. (2014) 'Gender and abortion attitudes: Religiosity as a suppressor variable', *Public Opinion Quarterly*, 78 (4): 940–50.

Barnard, S., Kim, C., Park, M.H. and Ngo, T.D. (2015) 'Doctors or mid-level providers for abortion', *Cochrane Database of Systematic Reviews*, CD011242.

Bartlett, L.A., Berg, C.J., Shulman, H.B., et al (2004) 'Risk factors for legal induced abortion-related mortality in the United States', *Obstetrics & Gynecology*, 103: 729–37.

BBC (2017) 'Lord Steel: we should decriminalise abortion', *BBC News*. Available from: www.bbc.co.uk/news/av/uk-politics-41683395/lord-steel-we-should-decriminalise-abortion [Accessed 31 October 2019].

Beauchamp, T.L. and Childress, J.F. (2013) *Principles of Biomedical Ethics*. New York: Oxford University Press.

Beynon-Jones, S.M. (2012) 'Expecting motherhood? Stratifying reproduction in 21st-century Scottish abortion practice', *Sociology*, 47: 509–25.

Bhattacharya, S., Lowit, A., Bhattacharya S., et al (2012) 'Reproductive outcomes following induced abortion: a national register-based cohort study in Scotland', *BMJ Open* 2: e000911.

Birkett (1939) *Report of the Inter-Departmental Committee on Abortion*. London: HMSO.

Bloomer, F., Pierson, C. and Estrada-Claudio, S. (2019) *Reimagining Global Abortion Politics*. Bristol: Policy Press.

BMA (British Medical Association) (2019) *How will Abortion be Regulated in the United Kingdom if the Criminal Sanctions for Abortion are Removed?* London: BMA.

Both Lives Matter (2019) 'Lucid Talk poll on abortion'. Available from: https://docs.wixstatic.com/ugd/024943_65bc35bf6cae4f0 58aabc5d74139924e.pdf [Accessed 31 October 2019].

Bracken, H., Dabash, R., Tsertsvadze, G., et al (2014) 'A two-pill sublingual misoprostol outpatient regimen following mifepristone for medical abortion through 70 days' LMP: a prospective comparative open-label trial', *Contraception*, 89: 181–86.

BSA (British Social Attitudes Survey) (2015) *Personal Relationships: Abortion*. Natcen Social Research, 30th edition. Available from: www.bsa.natcen.ac.uk/latest-report/british-social-attitudes-30/personal-relationships/abortion.aspx [Accessed 24 September 2019].

Carroll, R. (2018) 'Northern Irish woman to challenge abortion prosecution', *The Guardian*. Available from: www.theguardian.com/uk-news/2018/nov/05/northern-irish-woman-abortion-pills-fights-prosecution [Accessed 31 October 2019].

Carter, S., Carter, S. and Dodge, J. (2009) 'Trends in abortion attitudes by race and gender: a reassessment over a four-decade period', *Journal of Sociological Research*, ISSN 1948-5468 2009; 1 (1): E3.

Cates, W., Grimes, D.A. and Schulz, K.F. (2003) 'The public health impact of legal abortion: 30 years later', *Perspectives on Sexual and Reproductive Health*, 35: 25–8.

Caulfield, M. (2017) 'Reproductive Health (Access to Terminations)' [debate], House of Commons Debates Vol 623, 13 March. Available from: https://hansard.parliament.uk/commons/2017-03-13/debates/D76D740D-2DDD-4CCB-AC11-C0DBE3B7D0D8/ReproductiveHealth(AccessToTerminations) [Accessed 31 October 2019].

Clarke, L. (2012) 'Abortion: 45% want a liberalisation of the law in Northern Ireland', *Belfast Telegraph*, 30 November. Available from: https://www.belfasttelegraph.co.uk/news/northern-ireland/abortion-45-want-a-liberalisation-of-the-law-in-northern-ireland-28999931.html [Accessed 12 December 2019].

Clarke, L.(2014) 'SDLP leader Alasdair McDonnell fails to get endorsement from rank-and-file party activists – poll', *Belfast Telegraph*, 17 November. Available from: https://www.belfasttelegraph.co.uk/news/politics/sdlp-leader-alasdair-mcdonnell-fails-to-get-endorsement-from-rankandfile-party-activists-poll-30748879.html [Accessed 12 December 2019].

CCOPMM (Consultative Council on Obstetric and Paediatric Mortality and Morbidity) (2011) *Annual Report for the Year 2008, Incorporating the 47th Survey of Perinatal Deaths in Victoria*. Melbourne: State Government of Victoria.

CCOPMM (2012) *Annual Report for the Year 2009, Incorporating Births in Victoria and the 48th Survey of Perinatal Deaths in Victoria.* Melbourne: State Government of Victoria.

CCOPMM (2014) *2010 and 2011 Victoria's Mothers and Babies: Victoria's Maternal, Perinatal, Child and Adolescent Mortality.* Melbourne: State Government of Victoria.

CCOPMM (2016) *2012 and 2013 Victoria's Mothers, Babies and Children Section 2: Data, Tables and Figures.* Melbourne: State Government of Victoria.

CCOPMM (2017a) *Victoria's Mothers, Babies and Children 2014 and 2015.* Melbourne: State Government of Victoria.

CCOPMM (2017b) *Victoria's Mothers, Babies and Children 2016.* Melbourne: State Government of Victoria.

CEDAW (Committee on the Elimination of Discrimination Against Women) (2018) *Report of the Inquiry Concerning the United Kingdom of Great Britain and Northern Ireland under Article 8 of the Optional Protocol to the Convention on the Elimination of all Forms of Discrimination against Women* (CEDAW/C/OP.8/GBR/1), 6 March. https://undocs.org/CEDAW/C/OP.8/GBR/1 [Accessed 29 December 2019].

Chae, S., Desai, S., Crowell, M., et al (2017) 'Reasons why women have induced abortions: a synthesis of findings from 14 countries', *Contraception*, 96 (4): 233–41.

Chao, F., Gerland, P., Cook, A.R., et al (2019) 'Systematic assessment of the sex ratio at birth for all countries and estimation of national imbalances and regional reference levels'. Available from: www.pnas.org/cgi/doi/10.1073/pnas.1812593116 [Accessed 8 August 2019].

Chavkin, W., Swerdlow, L. and Fifield, J. (2017) 'Regulation of conscientious objection to abortion: an international comparative multiple-case study', *Health and Human Rights Journal*, 19: 55–68.

CIHI (Canadian Institute of Health Information) (2012) *Therapeutic Abortion Survey 2010: Notes on Data Quality.* Ottawa: Government of Canada. Available from: www.cihi.ca/CIHI-extportal/pdf/internet/TA_10_ALLDATATABLES20120417_EN [Accessed 22 March 2019].

CIHI (2014) *Induced Abortions Performed in Canada in 2012.* Ottawa: Government of Canada. Available from: www.cihi.ca/CIHI-ext-portal/pdf/internet/TA_11_ALLDATATABLES20140221_EN [Accessed 22 March 2019].

CIHI (2019) *Induced Abortions Reported in Canada in 2016.* Ottawa: Government of Canada. Available from: www.cihi.ca/sites/default/files/document/induced-abortion-can-2016-en-web.xlsx [Accessed 22 March 2019].

Clements, B. (2014) 'Religion and the sources of public opposition to abortion in Britain: the role of "belonging", "behaving" and "believing"', *Sociology*, 48 (2): 369–86

CMA (Canadian Medical Association) (1988) 'CMA policy summary. Induced abortion', *Canadian Medical Association Journal*, 139: 1176A–76B.

College of Nurses of Ontario (2017) 'What NPs should know about Mifegymiso'. Available from: www.cno.org/en/news/2017/july-2017/what-nps-should-know-about-mifegymiso/ [Accessed 24 March 2019].

College of Physicians and Surgeons of British Columbia (2019) *Practice Standards and Professional Guidelines.* Vancouver, BC. Available from: www.cpsbc.ca/for-physicians/standards-guidelines [Accessed 7 August 2019].

College of Physicians and Surgeons of Ontario (2019) 'About the College'. Available from: www.cpso.on.ca/About-Us [Accessed 25 March 2019].

ComRes (2017) 'A survey of British adults on behalf of "Where Do They Stand?" on abortion'. Available from: www.comresglobal.com/polls/where-do-they-stand-abortion-survey [Accessed 16 October 2019).

ComRes (2018) 'Both Lives Matter poll'. Available from: www.comresglobal.com/wp-content/uploads/2018/10/2018-Both-Lives-Matter.pdf

CQC (Care Quality Commission) (2018) *Inspection Framework: Independent Acute Hospitals (and Single Specialty). Core Service (or Single Specialty): Termination of Pregnancy* (V2.01). London: CQC.

David, H.P. (1974) 'Abortion and family planning in the Soviet Union: public policies and private behaviour', *Journal of Biosocial Science*, 6: 417–26.

David, H.P. (1981) 'Abortion policies', in J.E. Hodgson (ed) *Abortion and Sterilization: Medical and Social Aspects*. London: Academic Press.

David, H.P. (1992) 'Abortion in Europe, 1920–91: a public health perspective', *Studies in Family Planning*, 23 (1): 1–22.

Davis, A. (1950) '2,665 cases of abortion: a clinical survey', *British Medical Journal*, 2: 123–30.

Dawson, A.J., Nicolls, R., Bateson, D., et al (2017) 'Medical termination of pregnancy in general practice in Australia: a descriptive-interpretive qualitative study', *Reproductive Health*, 14: 39.

de Costa, C.M. and Douglas, H. (2015) 'Abortion law in Australia: it's time for national consistency and decriminalisation', *Medical Journal of Australia*, 203 (9): 349–50.

De Londras, F. (forthcoming) '"A hope raised and then defeated": the continuing harms of Irish abortion law', *Feminist Review*.

de Moel-Mandel, C. and Shelley, J.M. (2017) 'The legal and non-legal barriers to abortion access in Australia: a review of the evidence', *European Journal of Contraception and Reproductive Health Care*, 22 (2): 114–22.

Department of Justice (NI) (2015) *The Criminal Law on Abortion: Lethal Fetal Abnormality and Sexual Crime. Response to the Consultation and Policy Proposals* (April). Available from: https://www.justice-ni.gov.uk/consultations/consultation-abortion-2014 [Accessed 12 December 2019]

Department of Transport (2018) *Reported Road Casualties Great Britain, Annual Report: 2017*. London: Department for Transport.

Desmarais, L. (1999) *Mémoires d'une bataille inachevée: la lutte pour l'avortement au Québec, 1970–1992*. Montréal: Éditions trait d'union.

DGPSCF (Direction Générale des Programmes Service à la Condition Féminine) (1995) *Direction générale de la planification et de l'évaluation. Orientations ministérielles en matière de planification des naissances*. Quebec City, Canada: Ministère de la santé et des services sociaux.

DH (Department of Health) (2013) *Guidance: A Framework for Sexual Health Improvement in England.* Available from: www.gov.uk/government/publications/a-framework-for-sexual-health-improvement-in-england [Accessed 31 October 2019].

DH (2014) *Procedures for the Approval of Independent Sector Places for the Termination of Pregnancy (Abortion).* Available from: https://assets.publishing.service.gov.uk/government/uploads/system/uploads/attachment_data/file/313443/final_updated_RSOPs_21_May_2014.pdf [Accessed 29 December 2019].

DHSC (Department of Health and Social Care) (2018a) *Abortion Statistics, England and Wales: 2017.* London: Department of Health and Social Care. Available from: https://assets.publishing.service.gov.uk/government/uploads/system/uploads/attachment_data/file/808556/Abortion_Statistics__England_and_Wales_2018__1_.pdf [Accessed 4 December 2019].

DHSC (2018b) *The Abortion Act 1967: Approval of a Class of Places.* London: Department of Health and Social Care. Available from: https://assets.publishing.service.gov.uk/government/uploads/system/uploads/attachment_data/file/768059/Approval_of_home_use_for_the_second_stage of_early_medical_abortion.pdf [Accessed 4 December 2019].

DHSC (2019a) *Abortion Statistics, England and Wales: 2018.* Available from: https://assets.publishing.service.gov.uk/government/uploads/system/uploads/attachment_data/file/808556/Abortion_Statistics__England_and_Wales_2018__1_.pdf [Accessed 31 October 2019].

DHSC (2019b) *Sex Ratios at Birth in Great Britain: 2013 to 2017.* Available from: www.gov.uk/government/statistics/sex-ratios-at-birth-in-great-britain-2013-to-2017 [Accessed 31 October 2019].

DHSSPS (Department of Health Social Services and Public Safety, Northern Ireland) (2016) *Guidance for HSC Professionals on Termination of Pregnancy, Department of Health, 2016.* Available from: www.health-ni.gov.uk/publications/guidance-hsc-professionals-termination-pregnancy-northern-ireland [Accessed 31 October 2019].

Dickens, B. (1966) *Abortion and the Law.* Bristol: MacGibbon and Kee.

Dressler J., Maughn, N., Soon, J.A., et al (2013) 'The perspective of rural physicians providing abortion in Canada: qualitative findings of the BC Abortion Providers Survey (BCAPS)', *PLoS One*, 8: e67070.

Dunn, S., Wise, M. R., Johnson, L.M., et al (2011) 'Reproductive and Gynaecological Health', in A.S. Bierman (ed) *The POWER Report (Project for an Ontario Women's Health Evidence-Based Report)*, Vol 2. Available from: www.powerstudy.ca/power-report/volume2/reproductive-gynaecological-health [Accessed 8 August 2019].

Edvardsson, K., Axmon, A., Powell, R., et al (2018) 'Male-biased sex ratios in Australian migrant populations: a population-based study of 1 191 250 births 1999–2015', *International Journal of Epidemiology*, 47 (6): 2025–37.

Elcot, J. and McDonald, H. (2017) 'Northern Irish Women win access to free abortion as May averts rebellion', *The Guardian*, 29 June.

Endler, M., Cleeve, A. and Gemzell-Danielsson, K. (2019a) 'Online access to abortion medications: a review of utilization and clinical outcomes', *Best Practice & Research: Clinical Obstetrics and Gynaecology*. Available from: https://doi.org/10.1016/j.bpobgyn.2019.06.009 [Accessed 31 October 2019].

Endler, M., Lavelanet, A., Cleeve, A., et al, (2019b) 'Telemedicine for medical abortion: a systematic review', *BJOG*, 126(9): 1094–1102. Available from: https://doi.org/10.1111/1471-0528.15684 [Accessed 12 December 2019].

Erdman, J. and Johnson Jr, B.R. (2018) 'Access to knowledge and the Global Abortion Policies Database', *International Journal of Gynecology and Obstetrics*, doi: 10.1002/ijgo.12509.

Erdman, J., Gruben, V., Nelson, E. (2017) *Canadian Health Law and Policy* (5th edn). Toronto: Lexis-Nexis Canada.

Fehlberg, T., Rose, J., Guess, G.D., et al (2019) 'The surgical burden of disease and perioperative mortality in patients admitted to hospitals in Victoria, Australia: a population-level observational study', *BMJ Open*, 9: e028671, doi: 10.1136/bmjopen-2018–028671

Ferris, L.E., McMain-Klein, M., Colodny, N., et al (1996) 'Factors associated with immediate abortion complications', *Canadian Medical Association Journal*, 154: 1677–85.

Francome, C. (2004) *Abortion in the USA and the UK*. Aldershot: Ashgate.

Gallup (2019) *Abortion*. Available from: https://news.gallup.com/poll/1576/abortion.aspx [Accessed 31 October 2019].

Ganatra, B., Gerdts, C., Rossier, C., et al (2017) 'Global, regional, and subregional classification of abortions by safety. 2010–14: estimates from a Bayesian hierarchical model', *Lancet*, 390 (10110): 2372–81. doi: 10.1016/S0140-6736(17)31794-4.

Gaudu, S., Crost, M. and Esteria, L. (2013) 'Results of a 4-year study on 15,447 medical abortions provided by privately practicing general practitioners and gynecologists in France', *Contraception*, 87: 45–50.

Gemzell-Danielsson, K. and Kopp Kallner, H. (2014) 'Mid-level providers', in S. Rowlands (ed) *Abortion Care*. Cambridge: Cambridge University Press, pp. 219–26.

Gill, R. and Norman, W.V. (2018) 'Telemedicine and medical abortion: dispelling safety myths with facts', *mHealth*, 4: 3, doi: 10.21037/mhealth.2018.01.01

GMC (General Medical Council) (2007) *0–18 Years: Guidance for all Doctors*. London: GMC. Available from: https://www.gmc-uk.org/ethical-guidance/ethical-guidance-for-doctors/0-18-years [Accessed 12 December 2019].

GMC (2008) *Consent: Patients and Doctors Making Decisions Together*. London: GMC. Available from: https://www.gmc-uk.org/ethical-guidance/ethical-guidance-for-doctors/consent [Accessed 12 December 2019].

GMC (2012) *Protecting Children and Young People: The Responsibility of all Doctors*. London: GMC. Available from: https://www.gmc-uk.org/ethical-guidance/ethical-guidance-for-doctors/protecting-children-and-young-people [accessed 12 December 2019].

GMC (2013a) *Good Medical Practice*. London: GMC. Available from: https://www.gmc-uk.org/ethical-guidance/ethical-guidance-for-doctors/good-medical-practice [Accessed 12 December 2019].

GMC (2013b) *Personal Beliefs and Medical Practice*. Available from: www.gmc-uk.org/-/media/documents/personal-beliefs-and-medical-practice_pdf-58833376.pdf [Accessed 31 October 2019].

Gold, M. and Chong, E. (2015) 'If we can do it for misoprostol, why not for mifepristone?', *Contraception*, 92: 194–6.

Goodyear-Smith, F. and Buetow, S. (2001) 'Power issues in the doctor-patient relationship', *Health Care Analysis*, 9: 449–62.

Gordon, G.H. (1967) *The Criminal Law of Scotland*. Edinburgh: W. Green & Son.

Government of British Columbia (1994) *Realizing Choices: Report of the British Columbia Task Force on Access to Contraception and Abortion Services*. Victoria. BC: Government of British Columbia.

Government of Canada (1969) *Criminal Law Amendment Act, 1968-69*. Ottawa: Government of Canada. Available from: https://scc-csc.lexum.com/scc-csc/scc-csc/en/item/5076/index.do [Accessed 22 March 2019].

Government of Canada (1982) *Constitution Act, Canadian Charter of Rights and Freedoms, Ottawa: Government of Canada*. Available from: https://laws-lois.justice.gc.ca/eng/Const/page-15.html [Accessed 7 August 2019].

Gray, A.M, Horgan, G. and Devine, P. (2018) 'Do social attitudes to abortion suggest political parties in Northern Ireland are out of step with their supporters?', *ARK Feature*, 7. Available from: https://www.ark.ac.uk/ARK/sites/default/files/2018-06/Feature7.pdf [Accessed 12 December 2019].

Grimes, D.A. and Creinin, M.D. (2004) 'Induced abortion: an overview for internists', *Annals of Internal Medicine*, 140: 620–6.

Grossman, D. (2019) 'Telemedicine for medical abortion: time to move towards broad implementation', *BJOG*. Available from: https://doi.org/10.1111/1471-0528.15802 [Accessed 31 October 2019].

Grover, A. (2011) *Interim Report of the Special Rapporteur on the Right of Everyone to the Enjoyment of the Highest Attainable Standard of Physical and Mental Health A/66/254*. Available from: www.un.org/ga/search/view_doc.asp?symbol=A/66/254 [Accessed 31 October 2019].

Guskin, E. and Clement, S. (2019) 'Abortion support is the highest it's been in two decades as challenges mount', *The Washington Post*, 10 July. Available from: www.washingtonpost.com/politics/2019/07/10/abortion-support-is-highest-its-been-two-decades-two-decade-high-challenges-roe-mount [Accessed 14 August 2019].

Guthrie, K. (2010) 'Care closer to home', *Best Practice & Research: Clinical Obstetrics and Gynaecology*, 24: 579–91.

Hall, A. and Ransom, W.B. (1906) 'Plumbism from the ingestion of diachylon as an abortifacient', *BMJ* 1: 428.

Hardy, G., Benjamin, A. and Abenhaim, H.A. (2013) 'Effect of induced abortion on early preterm births and adverse perinatal outcomes', *Journal of Obstetrics and Gynaecology Canada*, 35: 138–43.

Harries, J., Cooper, D., Strebel, A., et al (2014) 'Conscientious objection and its impact on abortion service provision in South Africa: a qualitative study', *Reproductive Health*, 11 (1): 16, doi: 10.1186/1742-4755-11-16

Haynes, S. (2019) 'After 158 years U.K. lawmakers have voted to decriminalize abortion in Northern Ireland. The fight's not over yet', *Time*, 25 July. Available from: https://time.com/5634762/northern-ireland-abortion-law-impact/ [Accessed 31 October 2019].

Heller, R., Purcell, C., Mackay, L., et al, (2016) 'Barriers to accessing termination of pregnancy in a remote and rural setting: a qualitative study', *BJOG*, 123: 1684–91.

Hertog, E. and Iwasawa, M. (2011) 'Marriage, abortion, or unwed motherhood? How women evaluate alternative solutions to premarital pregnancies in Japan and the United States', *Journal of Family Issues*, 32 (12): 1674–99.

HM Government (2018) *Working Together to Safeguard Children*. London: HMG.

Horga, M., Gerdts, C. and Potts, M. (2013) 'The remarkable story of Romanian women's struggle to manage their fertility', *Journal of Family Planning and Reproductive Health Care*, 39: 2–4.

Horgan, G. (2019) 'The genie is out of the bottle: self-managed abortions in Northern Ireland using pills', *Ark Policy Brief*. Available from: www.ark.ac.uk/ARK/sites/default/files/2019-03/update127.pdf [Accessed 31 October 2019].

Horgan, G. and O'Connor, J.S. (2014) 'Abortion and citizenship rights in a devolved region of the UK', *Social Policy and Society*, 13 (1): 39–49.

Horgan, G., Gray A.M. and Morgan, L. (2019) 'Developing policy for a full reproductive health service in NI', *Ark Policy Brief*. Available from: www.ark.ac.uk/ARK/sites/default/files/2019-10/policybrief12.pdf [Accessed 31 October 2019].

House of Commons Science and Technology Committee (2007) *Scientific Developments Relating to the Abortion Act 1967 Volume II HC 1045-II.* Available from: www.publications.parliament.uk https://tbinternet.ohchr.org/Treaties/CEDAW/Shared%20Documents/GBR/INT_CEDAW_ITB_GBR_8637_E.pdf [Accessed 31 October 2019].

Hyland, P., Raymond, E.G. and Chong, E. (2018) 'A direct-to-patient telemedicine abortion service in Australia: retrospective analysis of the first 18 months', *Australian and New Zealand Journal of Obstetrics and Gynaecology*, 58: 335–40.

ICM (2017) *Abortion Documentary Survey.* Available from: www.icmunlimited.com/wp-content/uploads/2017/10/OlOm-Abortion-Documentary-v1.pdf [Accessed 31 October 2019].

Ipsos MORI (2006) *Attitudes to Abortion: Trends.* Available from: www.ipsos.com/ipsos-mori/en-uk/attitudes-abortion-trends [Accessed 14 August 2019].

Ipsos MORI (2011) *Public Attitudes Towards Abortion.* Available from: www.ipsos.com/ipsos-mori/en-uk/public-attitudes-towards-abortion [Accessed 14 August 2019].

ISD (Information Services Division Scotland) (2019) *Termination of Pregnancy: Year ending December 2018.* Edinburgh: ISD Scotland. Available from: https://www.isdscotland.org/Health-Topics/Sexual-Health/Abortions/ [Accessed 12 December 2019].

Jelen, T. (2015) 'Gender role beliefs and attitudes toward abortion: a cross-national exploration. Journal', *Journal of Research in Gender Studies*, 5(1): 11–22.

Jelinska, K. and Yanow, S. (2018) 'Putting abortion pills into women's hands: realizing the full potential of medical abortion', *Contraception*, 97:86–9.

Joffe, C. (2009) 'Abortion and medicine: a sociopolitical history', in M. Paul, E.S. Lichtenberg, L. Borgatta, et al (eds) *Management of Unintended and Abnormal Pregnancy.* Chichester: Wiley-Blackwell, 1–9.

Johnson, B.R., Horga, M., and Andronache, L. (1993) 'Contraception and abortion in Romania', *Lancet*, 341: 875–8.

Johnson, Jr, B.R., Lavelanet, A.F. and Schlitt, S. (2018) 'Global Abortion Policies Database: a new approach to strengthening knowledge on laws, policies, and human rights standards', *BMC International Health and Human Rights*, 18 (35). Available from: https://doi.org/10.1186/s12914-018-0174-2 [Accessed 8 August 2019].

Johnson, T.R., Harris, L.H., Dalton, V.K., et al (2005) 'Language matters: legislation, medical practice, and the classification of abortion procedures', *Obstetrics & Gynecology*, 105: 201–4.

Joseph, K.S., Liu, S., Rouleau, J., et al (2010) 'Severe maternal morbidity in Canada, 2003 to 2007: surveillance using routine hospitalization data and ICD-10CA codes', *Journal of Obstetrics and Gynaecology Canada*, 32: 837–46.

Kaposy, C. (2010) 'Improving abortion access in Canada', *Health Care Analysis*, 18: 17–34.

Keag, O., Norman, J. and Stock, J. (2018) 'Long-term risks and benefits associated with cesarean delivery for mother, baby, and subsequent pregnancies: systematic review and meta-analysis'. *PLoS Medicine*, 15: e1002494.

Keogh, L.A., Newton, D., Bayly, C., et al (2017) 'Intended and unintended consequences of abortion law reform: perspectives of abortion experts in Victoria, Australia', *Journal of Family Planning and Reproductive Health Care*, 43 (1): 18–24.

Keogh, L.A., Gillam, L., Bismark, M., et al (2019) 'Conscientious objection to abortion, the law and its implementation in Victoria, Australia: perspectives of abortion service providers', *BMC Medical Ethics*, 20: 11.

Kirkman, M., Rowe, H., Hardiman, A., et al (2009) 'Reasons women give for abortion: a review of the literature', *Archives of Women's Mental Health*, 12: 365.

Kohn, J.E., Snow, J.L., Simons, H.R., et al (2019) 'Medication abortion provided through telemedicine in four U.S. States', *Obstetrics & Gynecology*, 134: 343–50.

Kopp Kallner, H., Gomperts, R., Salomonsson, E., et al (2015) 'The efficacy, safety and acceptability of medical termination of pregnancy provided by standard care by doctors or by nurse-midwives: a randomized controlled equivalence trial', *BJOG*, 122: 510–517.

Küng, S.A., Darney, B.G, Saavedra-Avendaño, B., et al (2018) 'Access to abortion under the heath exception: a comparative analysis in three countries', *Reproductive Health*, 15: 107.

Lane, E.K. (1974a) *Report of the Committee on the Working of the Abortion Act Volume I Report*, Cmnd 5579. London: HMSO.

Lane, E.K. (1974b) *Report of the Committee on the Working of the Abortion Act Volume II Statistical Volume*, Cmnd 5579. London: HMSO.

Lavelanet, A.F., Schlitt, S., Johnson Jr, B.R., et al (2018) 'Global Abortion Policies Database: a descriptive analysis of the legal categories of lawful abortion', *BMC International Health and Human Rights*, 18 (44). Available from: https://doi.org/10.1186/s12914-018-0183-1 [Accessed 8 August 2019].

Lavrakas, P.J. (ed) (2008) 'Acquiescence response bias', in *Encyclopedia of Survey Research Methods*. London: Sage, doi: https://dx.doi.org/10.4135/9781412963947.n3 [Accessed 31 October 2019].

Law Commission (2015) *Offences against the Person: Modernising the Law on Violence*. Available from: www.lawcom.gov.uk/offences-against-the-person-modernising-the-law-on-violence/ [Accessed 31 October 2019].

Lewis, G. (2007) *The Confidential Enquiry into Maternal and Child Health (CEMACH). Saving Mothers' Lives: reviewing maternal deaths to make motherhood safer – 2003–2005. The Seventh Report on Confidential Enquiries into Maternal Deaths in the United Kingdom.* London: CEMACH.

Liu, N., Vigod, S.N., Farrugia, M.M., et al (2019) 'Physician procedure volume and related adverse events after surgically induced abortion: a population-based cohort study', *Canadian Medical Association Journal*, 191: E519–E528.

Lohr, P.A., Wade, J, Riley, L., et al (2010) 'Women's opinions on the home management of early medical abortion in the UK', *Journal of Family Planning and Reproductive Health Care*, 36: 21–5.

Loll, D. and Stidham Hall, K., (2019) 'Differences in abortion attitudes by policy context and between men and women in the World Values Survey', *Women & Health*, 59 (5): 465–80.

Lord, J., Regan L., Kasliwal A., et al (2018) 'Early medical abortion: best practice now lawful in Scotland and Wales but not available to women in England', *BMJ Sexual & Reproductive Health*, 44: 155–8.

Macdonald, G. (2017) 'Politicians are out of touch with the public on abortion', *The Times,* 24 May. Available from: www.thetimes. co.uk/article/politicians-are-out-of-touch-with-the-public-on-abortion-zpmznzv8k [Accessed 16 October 2019].

Magro Malosso, E.R., Saccone, G., Simonetti, B., et al (2018) 'US trends in abortion and preterm birth', *Journal of Maternal–Fetal and Neonatal Medicine*, 31: 2463–7.

Major, B., Appelbaum, M., Beckman, L., et al (2009) 'Abortion and mental health: evaluating the evidence', *American Psychologist,* 64: 863–90.

Martin, D., Miller, A.P., Quesnel-Vallee, A., et al (2018) 'Canada's universal health-care system: achieving its potential', *Lancet*, 391: 1718–35.

McDonagh, M. (2017) 'A new poll shows there is a good deal of unease with the current abortion law', *Spectator*, 21 May. Available from: https://blogs.spectator.co.uk/2017/05/new-poll-shows-good-deal-unease-current-abortion-law/ [Accessed 16 October 2019]

McDonald, H. (2016) 'Northern Ireland woman given suspended sentence over self-induced abortion', *The Guardian*, 4 April. Available from: www.theguardian.com/uk-news/2016/apr/04/northern-irish-woman-suspended-sentence-self-induced-abortion [Accessed 31 October 2019].

McGee, A., Jansen, M. and Sheldon, S. (2018) 'Abortion law reform: why ethical intractability and maternal morbidity are grounds for decriminalisation', *Australian and New Zealand Journal of Obstetrics and Gynaecology*, 58: 594–7.

McGuinness, S. and Montgomery, J. (2019) 'Abortion law reform in Northern Ireland'. Available from: https://legalresearch.blogs.bris.ac.uk/2019/10/abortion-law-reform-in-northern-ireland/ [Accessed 9 December 2019].

McKnorrie, K. (1985) 'Abortion in Great Britain: one act, two laws', *Criminal Law Review*, 475.

McLemore, M.R., Desai, S., Freedman, L., et al (2014) 'Women know best: findings from a thematic analysis of 5,214 surveys of abortion care experience', *Women's Health Issues*, 24 (6): 594–9.

Montgomery, J. (2015) 'Conscientious objection: personal and professional ethics in the public square', *Medical Law Review*, 23: 200–20.

Morrow, M. (Lord) (2019) 'NI (Executive Formation) Bill' [debate], House of Lords Debates Vol 799, 15 July. Available from: https://hansard.parliament.uk/lords/2019-07-15/debates/2B487CC4-0C99-444D-A23F-574AACBAFBCE/NorthernIreland(ExecutiveFormation)Bill [Accessed 31 October 2019].

Munk-Olsen, T., Laursen, T.M., Pedersen, C.B., et al (2011) 'Induced first-trimester abortion and risk of mental disorder', *The New England Journal of Medicine*, 364: 332–9.

Munk-Olsen, T., Laursen, T.M, Pedersen, C.B., et al (2012) 'First-time first-trimester induced abortion and risk of readmission to a psychiatric hospital in women with a history of treated mental disorder', *Archives of General Psychiatry*, 69: 159–65.

Narasimhan, M., Allotey, P. and Hardon, A. (2019) 'Self-care interventions to advance health and wellbeing: a conceptual framework to inform normative guidance', *BMJ*, 365: 1688.

Nebel, K. and Hurka, S. (2015) 'Abortion: finding the impossible compromise', in C. Knill, C. Adam, and S. Hurka (eds) *On the Road to Permissiveness? Change and Convergence of Moral Regulation in Europe*. Oxford: Oxford University Press.

Nevill, M. (2017) 'Access to late abortion must be protected', *Nursing Standard*, 31 (50): 27.

NICE (National Institute for Health and Care Excellence) (2019) *Abortion care. NICE Guideline [NG140]* Available from: https://www.nice.org.uk/guidance/NG140 [Accessed 31 October 2019].

NILT (Northern Ireland Life and Times) (2016) *Survey Results: Abortion Module*. Available from: https://www.ark.ac.uk/nilt/results/abortion.html [Accessed 12 December 2019].

NIO (Northern Ireland Office) (2019) *UK Government Guidance for Health Care Professionals in Northern Ireland on Abortion Law and Terminations of Pregnancy in the period 22 October to 20 March 2020 in relation to the Northern Ireland (Executive Formation etc) Act 2019*. Available from: https://assets.publishing.service.gov.uk/government/uploads/system/uploads/attachment_data/file/837166/Guidance_for_the_medical_profession_in_Northern_Ireland.pdf [Accessed 12 December 2019].

NISA (Northern Ireland Social Attitudes) (1990) *Survey Results*. Available from: https://www.ark.ac.uk/sol/surveys/gen_social_att/nisa/1990/website/ [accessed 12 December 2019].

NMC (Nursing and Midwifery Council) (2018) *The Code: Professional Standards of Practice and Behaviour for Nurses, Midwives and Nursing Associates*. London: NMC.

Noble, K. (2017) *Northern Ireland Police must Stop Intimidating Equality Activists*. Open Democracy. Available from: www.opendemocracy.net/en/5050/northern-ireland-police-equality-activists/2019 [Accessed 31 October 2019].

Norman, W.V. (2012) 'Induced abortion in Canada 1974–2005: trends over the first generation with legal access', *Contraception*, 85: 185–91.

Norman, W.V. and Downie, J. (2017) 'Abortion care in Canada is decided between a woman and her doctor, without recourse to criminal law', *BMJ*, 356: j1506.

Norman, W.V., Bergunder, J. and Eccles, L. (2011) 'Accuracy of gestational age estimated by menstrual dating in women seeking abortion beyond nine weeks', *Journal of Obstetrics and Gynaecology Canada*, 33: 252–7.

Norman, W.V., Brooks, M., Brant, R., et al (2014) 'What proportion of Canadian women will accept an intrauterine contraceptive at the time of second trimester abortion? Baseline data from a randomized controlled trial', *Journal of Obstetrics and Gynaecology Canada*, 36: 51–9.

Norman, W.V., Guilbert, E.R., Okpaleke, C., et al (2016) 'Abortion health services in Canada: Results of a 2012 national survey', *Canadian Family Physician*, 62: e209–17.

NPEU (National Perinatal Epidemiology) (2018) *MBRRACE-UK Reports*. Oxford: NPEU, University of Oxford.

ONS (Office for National Statistics) (2011) *The 20th Century Mortality Files*. Available from: https://webarchive.nationalarchives.gov. uk/20150908090558/www.ons.gov.uk/ons/publications/re-reference-tables.html?edition=tcm%3A77-215593 [Accessed 31 October 2019].

ONS (2016) *Conceptions in England and Wales: 2016*. Available from: www.ons.gov.uk/peoplepopulationandcommunity/ birthsdeathsandmarriages/conceptionandfertilityrates/bulletins/ conceptionstatistics/2016 [Accessed 31 October 2019].

ONS (2018) *Death Registrations Summary Tables: England and Wales 2017*. Available from: www.ons.gov.uk/ peoplepopulationandcommunity/birthsdeathsandmarriages/ deaths/datasets/deathregistrationssummarytablesenglandandwal esreferencetables [Accessed 31 October 2019].

ONS (2019a) *Conceptions in England and Wales: 2017*. Available from: www.ons.gov.uk/peoplepopulationandcommunity/ birthsdeathsandmarriages/conceptionandfertilityrates/bulletins/ conceptionstatistics/2017 [Accessed 31 October 2019].

ONS (2019b) *Homicide in England and Wales: Year Ending March 2018*. Available from: www.ons.gov.uk/peoplepopulationandcommunity/ crimeandjustice/articles/homicideinenglandandwales/year-endingmarch2018/pdf [Accessed 31 October 2019].

ONS (2019c) *Birth Characteristics in England and Wales: 2018*. Available from: www.ons.gov.uk/peoplepopulationandcommunity/ birthsdeathsandmarriages/livebirths/bulletins/birthcharacter-isticsinenglandandwales/2018 [Accessed 12 December 2019].

O'Rourke, C. (2016) 'Advocating abortion rights in Northern Ireland: local and global tensions', *Social & Legal Studies*, 25 (6) 716–40.

Parish, T.N. (1935) 'A thousand cases of abortion', *Journal of Obstetrics and Gynaecology of the British Empire*, 42: 1107–21.

Petrie, J. and Adams, S. (2017) 'BBC show which featured a debate on abortion is accused of ignoring a poll that showed most don't want a change in laws', *Mail on Sunday*, 22 October. Available from: www.dailymail.co.uk/news/article-5004873/BBC-ignored-poll-showing-UK-conservative-views-abortion.html [Accessed 24 September 2019]

Pew Research Fact Tank (2018) 'News in the numbers: in the US and Europe, women are about as likely as men to favor legal abortion', 14 December. Available from: www.pewresearch.org/fact-tank/2018/12/14/in-the-u-s-and-europe-women-are-about-as-likely-as-men-to-favor-legal-abortion/ [Accessed 12 September 2019].

PHE (Public Health England) (2015) *Guidance: Sexual and Reproductive Health and HIV: Applying All Our Health.* Available from: www.gov.uk/government/publications/sexual-and-reproductive-health-and-hiv-applying-all-our-health [Accessed 12 December 2019].

Popinchalk, A. and Sedgh, G. (2019) 'Trends in the method and gestational age of abortion in high-income countries', *BMJ Sex Reproductive Health*, 0: 1–9, doi: 10.1136/bmjsrh-2018–200149.

Porter, E. (1996) 'Culture, community and responsibilities: abortion in Ireland', *Sociology*, 30(2): 279–298.

Potts, M., Diggory, P. and Peel, J. (1977) *Abortion*. Cambridge: Cambridge University Press.

Pregnancy Outcome Unit (2018) '*Pregnancy Outcome in South Australia 2016*. Adelaide: Prevention and Population Health Branch, SA Health, Government of South Australia.

PRRI (Public Religion Research Institue) (2019) 'The state of abortion and contraception attitudes in all 50 states'. Available from: www.prri.org/research/legal-in-most-cases-the-impact-of-the-abortion-debate-in-2019-america/ [Accessed 12 September 2019].

Purcell, C. (2015) 'The sociology of women's abortion experiences: recent research and future directions', *Sociology Compass*, 9: 585–96.

Purcell, C., Cameron, S., Lawton. J., et al (2017) 'Self-management of first trimester medical termination of pregnancy: a qualitative study of women's experiences', *BJOG*, 124: 2001–8.

Räisänen, S., Gissler, M., Saari, I, et al (2013) 'Contribution of risk factors to extremely, very and moderately preterm births: register-based analysis of 1,390,742 singleton births', *PLoS One*, 8 (4): e60660, doi: 10.1371/journal.pone.0060660

Ralph, L.J., Schwarz E.B., Grossman, D., et al (2019) 'Self-reported physical health of women who did and did not terminate pregnancy after seeking abortion services: a cohort study', *Annals of Internal Medicine*, 11 June, https://doi.org/10.7326/M18-1666

Raymond, E.G. and Grimes, D.A. (2012) 'The comparative safety of legal induced abortion and childbirth in the United States'. *Obstetrics & Gynecology*, 119 (2, pt 1): 215–19.

Raymond, E., Chong, E., Winikoff, B., et al (2019) 'TelAbortion: evaluation of a direct to patient telemedicine abortion service in the United States', *Contraception*, 100 (3):173–7, https://doi.org/10.1016/j.contraception.2019.05.013

RCOG (Royal College of Obstetricians and Gynaecologists) (2010a) *Termination of Pregnancy for Fetal Abnormality in England, Scotland and Wales*. London: RCOG.

RCOG (2010b) *Fetal Awareness: Review of Research and Recommendations for Practice*. London: RCOG.

RCOG (2011) *The Care of Women Requesting Induced Abortion (Evidence-based Clinical Guideline No. 7)*. London: RCOG.

RCOG (2018) *Written Submission from Royal College of Obstetricians and Gynaecologists* (ANI0391). Available from: http://data.parliament. uk/writtenevidence/committeeevidence.svc/evidencedocument/ women-and-equalities-committee/abortion-law-in-northern-ireland/written/93765.html [Accessed 12 December 2019].

RCPCH (Royal College of Paediatrics and Child Health) (2014) *Safeguarding Children and Young People: Roles and Competences for Health Care Staff (Intercollegiate Document published by the Royal College of Paediatrics and Child Health 2014 on behalf of the contributing organisations* (3rd edn). London: RCPCH.

RCGP (Royal College of General Practitioners) (2011a) *Confidentiality and Young People Toolkit*. Available from: www.rcgp.org.uk/-/media/Files/CIRC/Safeguarding-Children/Confidentiality-Toolkit.ashx?la=en [Accessed 16 October 2019].

Regan, L. and Glasier, A. (2017) 'The British 1967 Abortion Act: still fit for purpose?', *Lancet*, 390: 1936–7.

Rooney, J. (2019a) 'Standing and the Northern Ireland Human Rights Commission', *Modern Law Review*, 82: 525–48.

Rooney, J. (2019b) 'Abortion in Northern Ireland: The Ewart Judicial Review Judgment'. Available from: https://legal-research.blogs.bris.ac.uk/2019/10/abortion-in-northern-ireland-the-ewart-judicial-review-judgment/ [Accessed 8 December 2019].

Rowlands, S. (2014) 'Longer-term outcomes', in S. Rowlands (ed) *Abortion Care*. Cambridge: Cambridge University Press.

Rowlands, S. and Walker, S. (2019) 'Reproductive control by others: means, perpetrators and effects', *BMJ Sexual & Reproductive Health*, 45: 61–7.

Sanhueza Smith, P., Peña M., Dzuba, I.G., et al (2015) 'Safety, efficacy and acceptability of outpatient mifepristone-misoprostol medical abortion through 70 days since last menstrual period in public sector facilities in Mexico City', *Reproductive Health Matters*, 22 (Suppl1): 75–82.

SCIE (Social Care Institute for Excellence) (2011) *Good Practice Guidance on Accessing the Court of Protection*. London: SCIE.

Science and Technology Committee (2007) *Scientific Developments Relating to the Abortion Act 1967 (Twelfth Report of Session 2006–7) Volume 1*, HC 1045-1.

Sedgh, G., Bearak, J., Singh, S., et al (2016) 'Abortion incidence between 1990–2014: global, regional, and subregional levels and trends', *Lancet*, 388 (10041): 258–67.

Shaw, D. and Norman, W.V. (2019) 'When there are no abortion laws: a case study of Canada', *Best Practice and Research Clinical Obstetrics and Gynaecology*. Available from: https://doi.org/10.1016/j.bpobgyn.2019.05.010 [Accessed 8 August 2019].

Sheldon, S. (2016) 'The decriminalisation of abortion: an argument for modernisation', *Oxford Journal of Legal Studies*, 36 (2): 334–65.

Singh, S., Remez, L., Sedgh, G., Kwok, L. and Onda, T. (2018) *Abortion Worldwide 2017: Uneven Progress and Unequal Access*. New York: Guttmacher Institute.

Smith, J.L. and Cameron, S. (2019) 'Current barriers, facilitators and future improvements to advance quality of abortion care: views of women', *BMJ Sexual & Reproductive Health*, 45: 207–12.

Statistics Canada (2019) *Population Estimates on July 1st, by Age and Sex, 1987 to 2016*. Ottawa: Government of Canada. Available from: https://www150.statcan.gc.ca/t1/tbl1/en/tv.action?pid=1710000501 [Accessed 25 March 2019].

Steinberg, J.R., Tschann, J.M., Furgerson. D. and Harper, C.C. (2016) 'Psychosocial factors and pre-abortion psychological health: the significance of stigma', *Social Science and Medicine*, 150: 67–75.

Stephenson, P., Wagner, M., Badea, M., et al (1992) 'The public health consequences of restricted induced abortion – lessons from Romania', *American Journal of Public Health*, 82 (10): 1328–31.

Swica, Y., Chong, E., Middleton, T., et al (2013) 'Acceptability of home use of mifepristone for medical abortion', *Contraception*, 88: 122–7.

Tamang, A., Puri, M., Masud, S., et al (2018) 'Medical abortion can be provided safely and effectively by pharmacy workers trained within a harm reduction framework: Nepal', *Contraception*, 97: 137–43.

Taylor, E.A. (2017) 'British attitudes to abortion', 3 August. Available from: www.bsa.natcen.ac.uk/media/39147/bsa34_moral_issues_final.pdf [Accessed 12 September 2019].

TNS Sofres (2005) 'European Values' [pdf], May. Commissioned by EURO RSCG. Paris: TNS Sofres. Available from: https://web.archive.org/web/20070619211339/www.thebrusselsconnection.be/tbc/upload/attachments/European%20Values%20Overall%20EN.pdf [Accessed 14 August 2019].

Trogstad, L., Magnus, P., Skjærven, R., et al (2008) 'Previous abortions and risk of pre-eclampsia', *International Journal of Epidemiology*, 37: 1333–40.

Ulster Marketing Surveys (1992) *Report on Abortion*. Belfast: Ulster Marketing Surveys.

United Nations Department of Economic and Social Affairs (2001–02) *Abortion Policies: A Global Review, Volumes 1–3*. New York: United Nations.

Urquhart, C. (2014) 'Woman accidentally kills herself after drinking vinegar to abort pregnancy', *The Guardian*, 6 March. Available from: www.theguardian.com/uk-news/2014/mar/06/woman-accidentally-kills-herself-drinking-vinegar-abort-pregnancy [Accessed 31 October 2019].

Urquia, M.L., Ray, J.G., Wanigaratne, S., et al (2016) 'Variations in male–female infant ratios among births to Canadian- and Indian-born mothers, 1990–2011: a population-based register study', *Canadian Medical Association Journal Open*, 4: E116–E123.

Vallance, W.B. (1955) 'Pennyroyal poisoning: a fatal case', *Lancet*, 269: 850–1.

Virk, J., Zhang, J. and Olsen, J. (2007) 'Medical abortion and the risk of subsequent adverse pregnancy outcomes', *The New England Journal of Medicine*, 357: 648–53.

VLRC (Victorian Law Reform Commission) (2008) *Law of Abortion* (Final Report 15). Melbourne: VLRC.

Wainwright, M., Colvin, C.J., Swartz, A., et al (2016) 'Self-management of medical abortion: a qualitative evidence synthesis', *Reproductive Health Matters*, 24: 155–67.

Warriner, I.K., Meirik, O., Hoffman, M., et al (2006) 'Rates of complication in first-trimester manual vacuum aspiration abortion done by doctors and mid-level providers in South Africa and Vietnam: a randomised controlled equivalence trial', *Lancet*, 368: 1965–72.

Weale, A., Bicquelet, A. and Bara, J. (2012) 'Debating abortion, deliberative reciprocity and parliamentary advocacy', *Political Studies*, 60 (3): 643–77.

Wellings, K., Jones, K.G., Mercer, C.H., et al (2013) 'The prevalence of unplanned pregnancy and associated factors in Britain: findings from the third National Survey of Sexual Attitudes and Lifestyles (Natsal-3)', *Lancet*, 382 (9907): 1807–16.

Wellings, K., Palmer, M.J., Geary, R.S., et al (2016) 'Changes in conceptions in women younger than 18 years and the circumstances of young mothers in England in 2000–12: an observational study', *Lancet*, 388 (10044): 586–95.

WHO (World Health Organization) (2011) *Preventing Gender-based Sex Selection: An Interagency Statement OHCHR, UNFPA, UNICEF, UN Women and WHO*. Geneva: World Health Organization. Available from: https://www.who.int/reproductivehealth/publications/gender_rights/9789241501460/en/ [Accessed 12 December 2019].

WHO (2012a) *Safe Abortion: Technical and Policy Guidance for Health Systems*. Geneva: World Health Organization. Available from: https://www.who.int/reproductivehealth/publications/unsafe_abortion/9789241548434/en/ [Accessed 12 December 2019].

WHO (2012b) *WHO Recommendations: Optimizing Health Worker Roles to Improve Access to Key Maternal and Newborn Health Interventions Through Task Shifting*. Geneva: World Health Organization. Available from: https://optimizemnh.org/optimizing-health-worker-roles-maternal-newborn-health/ [Accessed 12 December 2019].

WHO (2015) *Health Worker Roles in Providing Safe Abortion Care and Post-abortion Contraception*. Geneva: World Health Organization. Available from: https://www.who.int/reproductivehealth/publications/unsafe_abortion/abortion-task-shifting/en/ [Accessed 12 December 2019].

WHO (2018) *Global Abortion Policies Database*. Available from: https://abortion-policies.srhr.org/ [Accessed 24 July 2019].

WHO (2019) *WHO Consolidated Guideline on Self-care Interventions for Health*. Geneva: World Health Organization. Available from: https://www.who.int/reproductivehealth/publications/self-care-interventions/en/ [Accessed 12 December 2019].

Wiebe, E.R. and Sandhu, S. (2008) 'Access to abortion: what women want from abortion services', *Journal of Obstetrics and Gynaecology Canada*, 30: 327–31.

Wilcox, A.J., Treloar, A.E. and Sandler, D.P. (1981) 'Spontaneous abortion over time: comparing occurrence in two cohorts of women a generation apart', *American Journal of Epidemiology*, 114: 548–53.

Williams, A. (2017) 'Abortion show questioned by Christian MP', *Premier*, 22 October. Available from: www.premier.org.uk/News/UK/Abortion-show-questioned-by-Christian-MP [Accessed 31 October 2019].

Winikoff, B., Dzuba, I.G., Chong, E., et al (2012) 'Extending outpatient medical abortion services through 70 days of gestational age', *Obstetrics & Gynecology*, 120: 1070–6.

Women and Equalities Committee (2019) *Abortion Law in Northern Ireland: Eighth Report of Session 2017–19* (HC 1584). London: House of Commons.

Index

Notes: Page numbers in **bold** refer to tables and those in *italics* refer to figures. Page references for legal articles are listed in the table of cases, statutes and statutory instruments in the front of the book.